BEN'S
BARBECUE

BEN O'DONOGHUE
BEN'S BARBECUE

Hardie Grant Books

Published in 2009 by
Hardie Grant Books
85 High Street
Prahran, Victoria 3181, Australia
www.hardiegrant.com.au

Text © Ben O'Donoghue 2009
Photography © Craig Kinder 2009

Cataloguing-in-Publication data is available
from the National Library of Australia.

ISBN: 978 1 74066 807 1

Designed by Nanette Backhouse at Saso Content & Design
Food preparation: Ben O'Donoghue and Mandy Biffin
Food Stylist: Jane Hann
Props stylist: Adele Snyman
Typeset in ITC Stone
Printed and bound in China by C&C Offset Printing

The publisher would like to thank the following for their generosity in
supplying props for this book: Accoutrement, All Hand Made, Camargue,
Country Road, ICI ET LA, Mud Australia, My Island Home, Plenty,
Prop Stop, Star Trader, Top 3 by Design, The Bay Tree and
The Essential Ingredient.

10 9 8 7 6 5 4 3 2 1

Contents

INTRODUCTION 1

EQUIPMENT AND TIPS 4

Sauces and rubs 10

Breads and bites 40

Vegetables and salads 66

Fish and shellfish 106

Meat 136

Fruit and sweet things 188

Drinks 214

CHEF'S NOTES 226

INDEX 230

ACKNOWLEDGEMENTS 235

Thousands of years ago, one of our clever ancestors worked out how to make fire. We may consider this discovery a relatively simple act, but the means by which our hunter-gathering forebears kept themselves safe, warm and fed evolved over the millennia into a style of cooking that continues to touch every culture, bringing people together all around the globe.

Barbecuing is a cooking technique – some would say an art form – that can be performed just about anywhere: in restaurants and backyards, in parks, at beaches or on street corners. The basic requirements are so simple, a barbecue can be fashioned from just about any raw materials you have to hand. I have seen shopping trolleys, terracotta planter boxes, metal garbage cans, roof sheeting, plough wheels – you name it. If you can build a fire in it, on it or under it, then you can have a barbecue. Whether you're talking about the hangi pits of New Zealand and Polynesia, the braziers in Morocco's souks, the blazing heat of a gaucho's grill, the pit masters of the southern states of America, the barbecue kings of the Antipodes or the street stallholders of Asia, the common denominator is always fire.

Fire lends a desirable flavour to food, and often evokes happy childhood memories of building a bonfire and having a go at cooking something in the flames. I well remember going down to the beach on early-morning fishing expeditions with my friends, building a fire and throwing our fresh catch onto the coals, the charred results leaving us utterly replete.

This initial foray into cooking led me down my professional path, and it was these childhood memories, combined with my more recent global wanderings and discussions with taxi drivers, kitchen porters and fellow barbecue aficionados, that prompted me to write this book.

The origins of the word *barbecue* lie in the Caribbean with the indigenous Taino, whose *barabicu* was a form of pit cooking using green pimento tree branches and leaves, which imparted their flavour to the food. The word *barbacoa* was used by the Mesa American people of Mexico, and it is generally accepted that the word we use today made its way into popular usage via Texas, which was once part of Mexico.

In most parts of the world, to barbecue means to directly grill food over hot coals or gas. In the US, however, it refers to a form of slow, indirect cooking that's more in keeping with the tradition of pit cooking. Common to all methods is the fact that a barbecue is undeniably the most social and relaxing form of cooking and entertaining. According to the learned American gentleman Jonathan Daniels (1902–81), 'Barbecue is a dish which binds together the taste of both the people of the big houses and the poorest occupants of the back end of the broken-down barn.'

Barbecues not only cross social and economic barriers, they also break down geographical and cultural boundaries. Every nation around the world has a form of barbecue, or certain types of food that are specifically cooked on one.

With the advent of new fuels and construction materials, the modern barbecue has come a long way from that classic backyard feature the wood-burning barbecue, constructed from a couple of bricks and a rusty metal grill or a 44-gallon barrel cut in half with thick metal mesh thrown over the top. These days, the barbecues we cook on are the compact designer models, ideal for apartment dwellers; hooded gas barbecues, with all their bells and whistles; kettle barbecues, with their rounded, domed design and useful lid; and those ineffectual electric barbecues found in public parks and picnic areas.

This book is a celebration of the barbecue and its global idiosyncrasies. All the classics are here, along with recipes I've re-invented and my own personal favourites. I have cooked or eaten all of these fabulous recipes while exploring and enjoying the diversity of the barbecue world. I hope you enjoy them as much as I do.

Equipment and tips

The keys to a successful barbecue are preparation and some level of organisation. Whether you're attempting a major gastronomic event or just grilling a few steaks, there are a few things you need to remember.

Before you start thinking about whether you're doing T-bones, brisket, satay or squid, the first and most important thing to keep in mind is the golden rule: make sure you have enough fuel!

Other important rules when barbecuing are:

- never leave your post
- never hand the tongs to someone you can't trust
- when smoking, always remember: if you're looking, you're not cooking
- also when smoking, what you need is a thin stream of smoke, not a great big cloud!

There are two basic methods of cooking on a barbecue:

DIRECT GRILLING involves exposing food directly to the heat source, using a skewer, grill or griddle. It's generally a fast way of cooking, and some people in the barbecue world consider it heresy!

INDIRECT COOKING uses heat transfer via convection. Generally, the heat source is set away from the food, so it's a slower way to cook. Hot, smoky air passes through an enclosed container, whether using the hood of a gas barbecue, the lid of a kettle barbecue or, as in the US where this style of barbecuing is most common, an entire trailer converted into an oven that can hold a whole pig! Some barbecue experts consider the flavour and tenderness of meat cooked this way to be far superior to directly grilled meat.

Note that I've included icons in the recipes to indicate which process is required. Orange indicates high heat and yellow, lower heat.

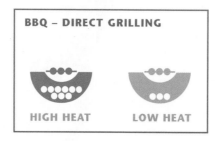

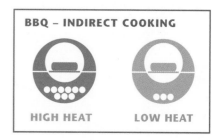

Fuel

The most popular barbecues on the market are the hooded gas and charcoal-fuelled kettle models, which can be used to cook either indirectly or directly. The main difference between gas and charcoal fuel is the fact that gas 'burns colder' than charcoal. This means it provides a lower cooking temperature than briquettes, charcoal or wood, which with the addition of oxygen (i.e. a fan) can burn hot enough to melt metals! Purists will say that the flavour gained from the use of charcoal is far superior, both in terms of smokiness and the high heat that's achieved to sear the meat. Gas, on the other hand, is cleaner and far more time efficient. Now that a range of woodchips for flavouring barbecues is available, the argument for coal over gas has no clear winner, the choice being merely one of tradition or modernity.

So, you have your hardware – now what else do you need? You'll probably have most of the following in your kitchen, but remember that preparation is everything and can make or break your barbecue.

- Enough fuel (gas, charcoal or briquettes)
- Lightweight long-handled tongs
- A roasting fork for turning large joints of meat and lifting delicate fish fillets
- A long-handled spatula with a cutting edge
- Leather or thick gloves for handling hot metal
- Oven or barbecue mitts
- Plenty of paper towels
- A selection of sharp knives: a 23 cm chef's knife for chopping, a long-bladed boning knife for boning and filleting fish and meat, and a paring knife for fruit and vegetables. And a diamond steel to keep them sharp!
- A basting needle or brush (needles are good because they don't singe)
- Long metal skewers for kebabs and trussing poultry and fish
- Wooden skewers (these need to be soaked in water for an hour before using, so they don't burn on the grill)
- A fish basket for grilling whole fish
- Foil or Qbags (an aluminium foil bag)
- Foil drip trays
- A roasting stand for large joints and birds
- A large, heavy cast-iron roasting tray
- A wire rack or cake rack to place over the roasting tray
- Selected woodchips (oak, mesquite, hickory, apple or your personal favourite), pre-soaked in water for an hour
- A bottle of water with a spray nozzle to help control woodchips when smoking
- A smoke box for giving your food that little extra touch of flavour when you're cooking with gas
- Absorbent material like fine gravel or kitty litter for the drip tray
- A fire extinguisher that's appropriate for the fire you're extinguishing – CO_2 is probably best
- A long-handled wire brush for cleaning
- Charcoal lighting chimney

Building your fire

Our hunter-gatherer ancestors had it tough. They had to carry fire with them while they travelled from one area to the next. What they would have given for a packet of firelighters and a box of Redheads!

The great convenience of gas is that you turn the bottle on, press the button and off you go. Gas barbecues need to heat up for 20–30 minutes, to help burn off any excess fat and dirt from the burners. Once clean, adjust the heat down a little and heat for a further 10 minutes for medium-hot; for medium–cool, reduce the heat a little more and heat for another 15 minutes. For simple grilling using gas, it's great to have high heat on one side graduating down to low on the other.

The ritual is slightly more involved if you have a charcoal barbecue. The fire needs to be built up and then allowed to burn down, requiring a preheating period of 35–45 minutes prior to cooking. A steady stream of fuel needs to be added during the cooking process, but the process of refuelling is not as simple as merely throwing more lumps of charcoal onto the fire. The smoke from coal is unclean when it initially starts to burn and can impart an unpleasant flavour to your barbecue. It's also hard to regulate the heat at first because in most cases the fire will cool prior to becoming hot again. The best way to maintain a constant heat using charcoal or briquettes is to use a fire box. It allows you to light new coals separately from your barbecue, quickly, evenly and efficiently, so when you add them they are hot enough to maintain your cooking temperature. Most modern coal barbecues have fire boxes.

With or without a fire box, the principle of lighting your coals is the same. Place your firelighters underneath your coals, so that the flames will rise up to light the coals evenly. The coals are ready for cooking when they are an even ashen white, which is when they are at their hottest. It takes up to 45 minutes to build an even coal base that is ashen white and hot enough to grill steaks or items that require fast high-heat cooking. Don't try to cook until the firelighters have burnt out or you will taint your food with the unpleasant fumes of accelerant. The way you arrange your coals will be determined by the method of cooking you wish to follow.

DIRECT GRILLING requires that you have a single base of evenly lit coals.

INDIRECT COOKING requires that you separate the coals into either a single heat source away from the cooking area (i.e. a heat box outside the kettle or hooded area of the barbecue, as is common in the US) or into two smaller heat sources on either side of the barbecue grill (this method is most commonly used in kettle barbecues), separated by a drip tray. Don't open the lid too often as the heat will escape. For indirect cooking using gas, turn your outside burners to medium–low and the inner burners off.

Adding water to the drip tray when indirect grilling will help maintain moisture within the meat being cooked. This can also be achieved by using a spray bottle of liquid – for extra flavour you could try adding a spirit such as bourbon, whisky or fruit juice.

Maintaining the heat

Sometimes it pays to build your fire so that it graduates from high intense heat to a lower, more controllable heat. This can be done by pushing more coals to one side and a few to the other. Also, the closer the grill to the heat source, the higher the cooking temperature.

Gas is pretty much the same in principle, although you are waiting for the gas to heat up the grill bars, which is dependent on how close they are to the heat. The great thing about gas is you can control the heat directly by adjusting it up and down.

Cleaning tips

Unfortunately, one thing that most barbecues suffer from is neglect. I gave my Scouser mate Jamie Grainger-Smith a barbecue, and every time I went around I would say to him, 'Mate, you've got to give this thing a clean!' Did he listen? Then one day, halfway through cooking his famous jerked chicken, the thing exploded into a ball of flames. A grease fire!

Always give your barbecue a good clean after you've used it. While the barbecue is still warm, use a long-handled wire-bristle brush and paper towels to remove charred material and fat from the grill plates and bars, then wash the surfaces down with hot soapy water. Next, allow the barbecue to burn for 10–15 minutes, to burn off any grease on the burners and grill tops. Change the absorbent material from the drip tray if it's excessively dirty.

When you come to use your barbecue again, give the grill bars and griddle plate another clean with a wire brush and paper towel. Importantly, prior to cooking you should allow your barbecue to burn very hot for a period (especially if it's gas) to burn off any debris or fat that may be left on the burners or hot rocks, as this may affect the flavour of your barbecue. I would also recommend a full strip down and a good deep clean at least once a year to prevent any serious fire accidents.

Kettle barbecues are a little easier to clean and maintain than gas. Most of the charcoal will burn to ash and will be caught in a tray underneath the bottom vents. The grill is easy to clean with a long-handled wire-bristle brush.

One thing both gas and kettle barbecues have in common is that neither of them like a lot of rain, so make sure you cover them when not in use.

SAUCES
AND RUBS

Sauces and rubs can define a barbecue,

taking a simple piece of meat, chicken or fish and transforming it into something sublime. Every table in every household in every corner of the world set up for a barbecue will have a sauce or seasoning on it. Just look at the humble tomato sauce – once a Chinese sauce, over time it has become an omnipresent condiment worldwide.

There are some fantastic sauces out there, too many to fit into one book, so I have focused on the ones that I love to use or that are associated with particular recipes, such as Gai Yang (page 165), barbecued chicken with sweet chilli sauce. They really are so easy to make, and once you know how, you won't buy readymade sauces ever again. They taste great and there are no surprises, as you know what's going in them.

Rubs and flavoured salts are really groovy things to use, whether as a dry marinade to impart flavour, as a curing agent to help draw out moisture and intensify flavours, or in order to tenderise meats. They too are easy to make and they keep well if stored in airtight containers. Here, you really know what you're getting when you make your own, as most shop-bought rubs and flavoured salts have major preservatives in them.

Basic barbecue sauce

No self-respecting American pit master would be caught behind a barbecue without a barbecue sauce recipe, and this one's both a sauce and a glaze. I brush it over barbecued ribs or pork belly in the final stages of cooking to create a glaze, but you can also use it as a straight barbecue sauce with grilled meats or sausages.

This basic recipe is a simple combination of sweet and sour components that works really well. If you'd like to try something a little different, experiment with fruit juices and other spices to mix it up a little. It's all about personal tastes.

MAKES 485 G

1 cup dark brown sugar

250 ml sherry vinegar
(preferably aged)

1 medium onion, chopped

1 teaspoon powdered cumin

½ teaspoon cinnamon

1 star anise

1 jalapeño chilli, halved

2 teaspoons smoked paprika

3 tablespoons tomato sauce

200 g canned chopped tomatoes

1 tablespoon salt

Combine all the ingredients in a heavy-bottomed saucepan.

Bring to the boil then reduce to a low simmer and cook for 30 minutes.

Use a stick blender to purée until the sauce is smooth. If the sauce is still thin, continue to cook it until the sauce coats the back of a spoon well.

Serve at room temperature. It will keep for up to 3 months in the refrigerator if stored in an airtight container.

Orange and ginger ketchup

One of my sous chefs came up with this great variation on that old favourite tomato sauce. It's great with barbecued duck, in particular, and also with scallops or prawns. Historically, tomato sauce is a Chinese sauce that was popularised by the Americans, so this combo makes a lot of sense.

MAKES 250 ML

250 ml tomato sauce

zest and juice (strained) of
   1 orange

1 teaspoon finely minced ginger

½ teaspoon dark sesame oil

Combine the tomato sauce with the orange zest and juice.

Add the ginger and sesame oil, and mix thoroughly.

Allow the tomato sauce to stand for 30 minutes before using.

Use this sauce on the same day.

Anchovy and rosemary sauce

I first came across the recipe for this Italian sauce at the River Café in London, and it epitomises the simple, big flavours of Italian cooking. It is the perfect accompaniment to grilled meat and fish, and absolutely wonderful on vegetables, especially broccoli and asparagus. I also like to use it as a rub for roasting legs of lamb, but with a lot less olive oil.

In my experience, people who don't normally like anchovies find this recipe a great introduction to their flavour, as the balance of lemon and rosemary diminishes the fishiness. Give it a go, you will love it!

SERVES 4

8 anchovy fillets, rinsed

juice of 2 lemons

½ teaspoon finely chopped
   rosemary leaves

160 ml extra-virgin olive oil

Pound or chop the anchovy fillets into a paste.

Mix in the lemon juice to make a creamy paste, then add the rosemary.

Spoon in the olive oil to create a semi-emulsion.

Best used straightaway. It will keep for up to 3 days in the refrigerator if stored in an airtight container.

Salsa verde

This all-time classic Italian sauce pairs perfectly with grilled meat, fish, poultry and vegetables. Key elements are really good extra-virgin olive oil, fresh herbs and good vinegar; you can also use lemon juice.

A tip for making a great salsa verde is to use a sharp knife or to have a sharp blade in your food processor, so the herbs are cut and not bruised.

MAKES 300 ML

1 cup flat-leaf or curly parsley
1 cup basil leaves
1 cup mint leaves
1 cup rocket
2 tablespoons capers
6 anchovy fillets
1 garlic clove, peeled
1½ tablespoons white wine vinegar
½ tablespoon Dijon mustard
185 ml extra-virgin olive oil
salt
freshly ground black pepper

Place the herbs in a food processor with the capers, anchovies and garlic, and process until finely chopped. If necessary, add the vinegar to loosen the mixture.

Spoon the mix into a bowl and stir in the mustard and olive oil. Combine completely, then season with pepper and salt.

Allow the salsa to stand for 30 minutes before using. Serve at room temperature.

The sauce will keep for up to 1 week in the refrigerator if stored in an airtight container.

1 Chimichurri
2 Anchovy and rosemary sauce
3 Aioli
4 Mexican spicy green sauce
5 Satay sauce
6 Nuoc cham
7 Harissa
8 Salsa di dragoncella

Chimichurri

This South American barbecue sauce is used right across the continent, from the southern Pampas regions to as far north as Honduras. It has as many variations as, say, the Italian salsa verde, but in its purest form it is just dried oregano, vinegar, chilli flakes, black pepper and olive oil. I like to use a combination of fresh and dried herbs because of their different characteristics.

In South America this recipe is used specifically for grilled meats (i.e. the perfect steak) but you can also spoon it liberally over chicken or fish. The South Americans don't go in for fancy rubs and marinades – it's all about the MEAT.

If possible, use dried wild oregano flowers to make this sauce – they're far more aromatic than just oregano.

MAKES 250 ML

1 tablespoon dried wild oregano flowers or dried oregano

2 tablespoons finely chopped oregano or sweet marjoram leaves

3 garlic cloves, finely chopped

3 shallots, finely chopped

½ teaspoon dried chilli flakes

½ teaspoon coarsely ground black pepper

3 tablespoons white wine vinegar

120 ml extra-virgin olive oil

salt

Rub the oregano flowers between your fingers to break them up. Combine with the chopped fresh herbs.

Add the garlic, shallots, chilli flakes and pepper. Pour in the white wine vinegar, combine and let stand for 10 minutes.

Stir in the olive oil and season with salt to taste.

This sauce is best used straightaway, as the acidity of the vinegar overpowers the freshness of the herb flavours if kept for too long.

Salsa di dragoncella

For me, this is like a béarnaise sauce, only a lot better for you! It is fantastic with boiled meats, fish and vegetables, and would be perfect served with Bistecca alla Fiorentina (page 146–7) or any barbecued steak.

MAKES 300 G

6 eggs
100 g 2–3-day-old ciabatta, crust removed
3 tablespoons white wine vinegar
1 cup chopped tarragon leaves
6 anchovy fillets, chopped
1 tablespoon chopped salted capers
salt
freshly ground black pepper
120 ml extra-virgin olive oil

Put the eggs in a pan of cold water, bring to the boil and simmer for 10 minutes until hard-boiled. Place the eggs under running cold water until cool enough to handle, then shell them. Discard the egg whites and chop the yolks.

Soak the stale bread in a little warm water until soft. Add the vinegar, and once soft squeeze the excess moisture from the bread and mash with a fork to break it up.

Add the tarragon, anchovies, capers and egg yolks, and combine. Season with salt and pepper, then add the olive oil. Allow to rest for 20–30 minutes before using.

This sauce is best used straightaway, served at room temperature. It will keep for 2 days in the refrigerator if stored in an airtight container.

Harissa

Harissa originates from Tunisia but it's commonly found throughout North Africa. It is a wonderful condiment to accompany barbecued lamb, or traditional lamb kofte, and goes well with grilled fish. Harissa also makes a great marinade for chicken and oily fish like mackerel, and is used to make salad dressings.

MAKES 160 G

½ teaspoon cumin seeds

1 teaspoon sea salt

1 large garlic clove, peeled

5 long red chillies, stems removed and roughly chopped

2 tablespoons white wine vinegar

1 tablespoon extra-virgin olive oil

Place the cumin seeds and sea salt in a mortar and pound to combine.

Add the garlic and pound to a paste.

Add the chopped chillies and continue pounding.

Pour in the white wine vinegar, followed by the olive oil, and pound until combined.

This sauce is best used straightaway and can be made as and when it's needed. It will keep for up to 1 week if stored in an airtight container. When re-using, allow the sauce to come back to room temperature.

Ssamjang

A Korean staple, ssamjang is a sauce is made from a mixture of kochujang, a chilli pepper paste, and dwenjang, a fermented soybean paste. Both pastes are available from Korean supermarkets or speciality Asian stores, and you can also buy ssamjang readymade. It is used as a condiment with barbecued meats, which are then wrapped in lettuce with fresh herbs, and it can be added to stir-fries or used as a marinade for ribs. I use this sauce to accompany Korean Daegi Bulgogi (page 182).

MAKES 425 G

80 ml kochujang

125 ml dwenjang

1 tablespoon finely chopped birdseye chillies

1 tablespoon finely chopped green pepper or capsicum

6 garlic cloves, peeled

½ tablespoon sesame seeds

2 tablespoons rice wine vinegar

1 tablespoon sesame oil

Place all the ingredients in a food processor and purée until smooth.

The sauce will keep for up to 3 weeks in the refrigerator if stored in an airtight container.

Miso marinade

This recipe is both a base for sauces and dressings, and a marinade for fish and chicken. Add it to Mayonnaise (page 30) or combine with wasabi, rice vinegar and oil for a fantastic dressing. This marinade is used in the Miso-blackened Fish Fillets (page 116) and robatayaki-style Miso Eggplant (page 73).

MAKES 500 G

500 g white miso paste

250 ml mirin

½ cup caster sugar

Combine the ingredients and place the mixture in a glass bowl suspended over a simmering saucepan of water. Leave it to cook for 1 hour, until the sugar has completely dissolved.

Allow to cool, then use as a marinade.

The marinade will keep for up to 1 month in the refrigerator if stored in an airtight container. It also freezes really well.

1 Orange and ginger ketchup
2 Thai sweet chilli jam
3 Miso marinade
4 Sweet chilli sauce
5 Classic barbecue sauce
6 Ssamjang

Mexican spicy green sauce

The recipe for this great sauce was given to me by a Mexican waiter at Monte's in London when I was head chef there. I use it to accompany Mexican barbecue dishes, such as Mexican Suckling Pig Tortillas (page 186). It also works well when strained and served with raw fish as a dipping sauce.

MAKES 250 ML

4 shallots
4 green chillies, seeded
100 ml lime juice
100 ml white wine vinegar or rice vinegar
2 tablespoons chopped coriander leaves
1 garlic clove, peeled

Combine all the ingredients in a food processor and purée into a medium-textured sauce.

Use straightaway. This sauce can't be stored for too long as the colour starts to fade after a few hours.

Sweet chilli sauce

Sweet chilli sauce exploded onto the food scene some ten or fifteen years ago, and became a gastro-pub staple served with chunky chips and sour cream. It shows how versatile the sauce is, and how popular it has become. It's the perfect accompaniment to the Thai barbecued chicken dish Gai Yang (page 165), and also works well with barbecued seafood – prawns, scallops or lobster.

If you prefer a milder sauce, use eight rather than fifteen chillies!

MAKES 600 ML

500 g caster sugar
500 ml white wine vinegar
500 ml water
4 lemongrass stems, peeled and finely sliced
10 garlic cloves, peeled
15 long red chillies, chopped
½ teaspoon salt

Combine the sugar, vinegar and water in a saucepan and bring to the boil.

Place the lemongrass, garlic, chillies and salt in a food processor and purée to a fine texture.

Add the paste to the saucepan, then simmer and reduce by half. Skim off any floating bits or any foam that forms.

Once thick, set aside to cool.

The sauce will keep for up to 2 months in the refrigerator if stored in an airtight container.

Thai sweet chilli jam

This sophisticated version of sweet chilli sauce is fantastic served with grilled scallops and prawns or smeared over whole barbecued fish or pork ribs. It's somewhat complicated to make but worth the effort.

MAKES 535 G

500 ml sunflower oil

125 g garlic, sliced lengthwise

250 g Thai pink shallots, sliced lengthwise

½ cup dried shrimps, rinsed in hot water and drained

8 dried long red chillies

125 g palm sugar

75 g tamarind paste

1 tablespoon fish sauce

salt

Heat 375 ml of the oil in a wok or large saucepan and fry the garlic and shallots separately until lightly golden, then remove and drain. Be careful, as they will continue to cook and darken once removed from the oil.

Fry the shrimps and chillies until fragrant, then remove and drain.

Purée the fried ingredients with 125 ml of the oil to form a paste. Transfer to a saucepan and bring to the boil.

Add the palm sugar, tamarind paste and fish sauce. Season with salt and simmer for 2–3 minutes until thick.

The sauce will keep for up to 1 week in the refrigerator if stored in an airtight container.

Satay sauce

This sauce is a staple of many South-East Asian countries, from Malaysia to Thailand, but it originally came from Java.

I love peanut butter, so it follows that I should love satay sauce. Its mild spicy flavour goes with just about anything, but chicken and beef are common choices. It matches perfectly with Malay Satay Beef (page 149), or use it as a sauce with barbecued chicken or over a grilled steak.

MAKES 250 ML

1 medium red chilli

2 tablespoons chopped coriander leaves

2 tablespoons crunchy peanut butter

2 tablespoons soy sauce

150 ml coconut milk

juice of ½ lime

Pound the chilli and coriander in a mortar to make a paste.

Add the peanut butter and combine.

Stir in the remaining ingredients, then transfer to a saucepan.

Bring to the boil and simmer until thick.

Use straightaway. This sauce doesn't keep too well, as it tends to set when it cools and will separate if reheated. It tastes so great, there probably won't be any left over anyway.

Nuoc cham

This dipping sauce tastes absolutely fantastic and adds a light sweet–sour flavour to Vietnamese barbecued dishes. It's traditionally used to dress Bun Bo (page 157) and also as a dressing for most Vietnamese salads.

MAKES 250 ML

5 tablespoons caster sugar

3 tablespoons water

80 ml fish sauce

juice of 3 limes

1 large or 2 small garlic cloves, finely minced

1 long red chilli or 2 birdseye chillies if you like heat

Whisk the sugar with the water.

Add the fish sauce and lime juice, and stir to dissolve the sugar completely.

Add the garlic and chilli and combine.

Allow the sauce to rest for 1 hour before serving.

The sauce will keep for up to 2 weeks in the refrigerator if stored in an airtight container.

Shallot and coriander salsa

This is the Mexican equivalent of an Indian raita, and makes a refreshing antidote to the heat of some of the chilli sauces served with a Mexican *barbacoa*. I serve this with my Mexican Suckling Pig Tortillas (page 186), but it's equally good with the Whole Fish Thai-Style (page 110) or Barbecued Pepper Chicken Curry (page 173).

MAKES 200 G

2 cups white salad onions, finely sliced

2 tablespoons chopped coriander leaves

1 green capsicum, finely diced

juice of 1 lime

freshly ground black pepper

Combine the salad onions, coriander and sweet pepper.

Squeeze the lime juice over the salsa and season with a pinch of pepper.

Serve straightaway. This salsa doesn't keep well.

Mayonnaise

Where would we be without this staple dressing for most backyard barbecues? Mayonnaise is just perfect on a burger, in a potato salad – you name it, this popular dressing can find a home on anything. But mayonnaise can be so much more than the white creamy dressing we all know and love. Different oils can take it in different directions and any number of other ingredients can be added to it to lift it to greater glory.

The type of oil you use depends on how you want to use the mayonnaise. Extra-virgin olive oil will give you a powerful taste that might not suit the subtle flavours of some fish, for example. Again, it comes down to personal taste.

I love to serve the basil mayo with barbecued fish. You could also use it in Coleslaw (page 101) instead of Greek yoghurt.

MAKES 600 ML

3 large egg yolks

salt

½ tablespoon Dijon mustard

1 teaspoon white wine vinegar

1 teaspoon water

500 ml vegetable oil or extra-virgin olive oil

freshly ground black pepper

juice of ½ lemon

Place the egg yolks, a good pinch of salt, the mustard, vinegar and 1 teaspoon of water in a bowl. Whisk to combine and aerate for 1–2 minutes.

Wet a tea towel, then roll it up and wind it around the base of the bowl to secure it, leaving your hands free to whisk and pour.

Pour the oil into the egg mixture in a thin but steady stream, whisking continuously. Stop for a little if your hand and arm become tired. Continue pouring and whisking until all the oil is added.

If the mixture is thick and too gluggy, thin it with a little water.

Season the mayonnaise with salt and pepper and a squeeze of lemon juice.

Use straightaway. Any leftover mayo will keep for 1 week in the refrigerator if stored in an airtight container.

Basil mayonnaise

1 cup basil leaves
pinch of salt
1 quantity Mayonnaise (opposite),
   made with extra-virgin olive oil
squeeze of lemon juice

Pound the basil with the salt to form a fine paste, then add to the mayonnaise and stir.

Correct the seasoning with a squeeze of lemon juice.

Aioli

3 garlic cloves, peeled
pinch of salt
1 quantity Mayonnaise (opposite)
squeeze of lemon juice

Pound the garlic with the salt to form a paste.

Combine the garlic with the mayonnaise and correct the seasoning with a squeeze of lemon juice.

Marie Rose cocktail sauce

100 ml tomato sauce
1 tablespoon Worcestershire sauce
½ tablespoon brandy
1 quantity Mayonnaise (opposite)
salt
freshly ground black pepper

Add the tomato sauce, Worcestershire sauce and brandy to the mayonnaise and combine.

Correct the seasoning with salt and pepper.

Guacamole

This salsa goes so well with barbecued pork or chicken, and especially with spicy food. It's the perfect accompaniment to the adobo-marinated Mexican Suckling Pig Tortillas (page 186). You can also serve it as a dip with plain tortillas or as a general addition to your barbecue.

I think the creamy flesh of dark-skinned Hass avocados is best suited to making guacamole. Ripe red tomatoes are fine for this recipe if good green varieties are unavailable.

SERVES 4

2 Hass avocados, halved, peeled and stone removed

1 jalapeño chilli, seeded and chopped

juice of 2 limes

2 shallots, finely diced

1 green tomato, seeded and chopped

1 tablespoon chopped coriander leaves and stems

salt

freshly ground black pepper

Roughly mash the avocados with a fork.

Add the remaining ingredients and roughly combine.

Guacamole is best served straightaway. It won't go off if you keep it for a day or 2 in the refrigerator, but it may change colour to an unpleasant brown!

Classic barbecue rib rub

We owe the Americans a great deal of thanks when it comes to barbecuing and the use of rubs. Pork has always been the mainstay of the American barbecue (well, except in Texas) and the rub is what defines a great piece of barbecued pork, along with a good deal of smoke and love. Whether it's ribs, belly, shoulder, neck or chops – you name it, pork loves this treatment.

MAKES ENOUGH FOR 1 SHOULDER OF PORK, 1 BELLY OR 3–4 RIB RACKS

3 tablespoons smoked paprika

6 tablespoons soft brown sugar

1 tablespoon Chipotle Salt (page 37)

2 tablespoons Celery Salt (page 35)

1 teaspoon ground ginger

2 teaspoons whole black peppercorns

1 teaspoon mustard powder

1 teaspoon onion flakes

1 teaspoon garlic flakes

Place all the ingredients in a small food processor and grind until fine. You could also use a mortar and pestle.

The rub will keep for 1 month if stored in an airtight container.

Celery salt

This is one of my favourite flavoured salts. It's a great way to use up all those dark green celery leaves that most people throw away. Celery salt adds wonderful flavour to fish, poultry and grilled meats, and it's also superb in rub recipes. I make a legendary Bloody Mary thanks to this secret ingredient!

When making any flavoured salt, it's imperative that you start with a top-quality salt. I always use coarse rock salt.

MAKES 165 G

2 cups dark celery leaves

1 cup coarse rock salt

1 teaspoon celery seeds (optional)

Wash the celery leaves and spin dry or allow to drain well.

Place the leaves in a large mortar, along with ½ cup of salt. Use a grinding motion to form a paste, which may be quite wet at first.

Add up to a ¼ cup of salt and grind until the paste is just moist and the leaves are well ground into the salt; you may not need to add a full ¼ cup of salt. The salt should be a nice pale to medium green colour, depending on the darkness of the leaves.

Line an oven tray with baking paper. Add the celery seeds to the salt (if using) then spread the mix evenly over the paper and place in a cool 100°C oven for around 1 hour, until completely dry.

The salt will keep for 1 month if stored in an airtight container or re-usable grinder.

Cajun spice

Cajun food was the big thing when I was an apprentice chef in the late 1980s, and we used to make our own spice mixture. We'd mix it with flour to deep-fry squid, dredge fish fillets through it prior to pan-frying and rub it onto pork. I particularly like to use this recipe as a base to make a rub for pork ribs or pork belly. Mix three parts Cajun spice to one part sugar and one part salt, then rub it all over the meat.

When I'm making dried herbs, I like to pick or buy fresh herbs then tie them together at their stems and hang them up to dry. Once they are dry, place them in an airtight container and they will last for up to a month. It's a great way to get the most out of your herbs.

MAKES 130 G

500 ml sunflower oil

1 large onion, finely sliced

10 garlic cloves, finely sliced

1 tablespoon cayenne pepper

1 tablespoon smoked paprika

1 tablespoon Celery Salt
    (page 35)

1 tablespoon dried thyme

1 teaspoon fennel seeds

Heat the oil in a wok. It needs to be *hot*! It should be about 150°C, or able to cook a slice of bread to a golden colour in 20 seconds.

Cook the onion and garlic separately, moving them around constantly so they cook evenly. Remove them from the heat when they start to turn a light golden colour, and place them on paper towels to cool and drain. You'll notice they will continue to colour.

Place the drained and cool fried onion and garlic in a hand-held food processor, along with the remaining ingredients, and blitz to a rough powder.

The spice will keep for 1 month if stored in an airtight container.

Cajun rub

Add 1 tablespoon soft brown sugar or palm sugar and 1 tablespoon salt to 3 tablespoons Cajun spice. Rub into the meat you are using and allow to marinate. The length of marinating time depends on the size of the joint or meat to be cooked; steaks or pork fillets will need 10–15 minutes, ribs maybe 30 minutes, and a beef brisket will need to be marinated overnight.

Chipotle salt

This funky salt works well in rubs and as a seasoning. You get the heat of the jalapeño chilli plus a smoky flavour because chipotles are smoked jalapeño chillies!

This salt is great on steaks, fish or pork, or for seasoning your classic Mexican adobo marinade for Suckling Pig Tortillas (page 186).

MAKES 250 G

8 chipotle chillies
1 cup coarse rock salt

Toast the chipotle chillies in a hot pan for 1–2 minutes. Remove the stems and seeds, then soak the chillies in 250 ml boiling water for 10 minutes.

Drain, then place the chillies in a large mortar, along with ½ cup of salt, and grind to a rough paste. Add the remaining salt and grind a little more.

Line an oven tray with baking paper. Spread the salt evenly over the paper and place in a cool 100°C oven for around 1 hour, until completely dry.

The salt will keep for 1 month if stored in an airtight container.

Garlic, lemon and green peppercorn salt

The great thing about salt is that it absorbs flavours so well. I fell in love with the practice of making my own salt when I was running the kitchen at Monte's in London, as sometimes it's nice to have something a bit different to grind onto a piece of fish or meat before you throw it onto the coals. Try this seasoning on Beer-Can Chicken (page 174) roasted on the barbecue, whole grilled fish or whatever takes your fancy!

MAKES 150 G

4 garlic cloves, thinly sliced

1 unwaxed lemon, thinly sliced

10 dried lemon verbena leaves

1 tablespoon dried green peppercorns

1 cup coarse rock salt

Line an oven tray with baking paper.

Arrange the slices of garlic and lemon on the paper, making sure they are lying flat.

Place the tray in a cool 100°C oven and leave to dry until crisp. This may take 1 hour for the garlic and up to 2 hours for the lemon.

Break the dried lemon and garlic into a bowl, along with the lemon verbena leaves.

Roughly crush the green peppercorns and add to the bowl.

Add enough salt to achieve an equal amount of dried ingredients and salt, and combine well.

The salt will keep for 1 month if stored in an airtight container or re-usable grinder.

Smoked salt and rosemary

Whoever thought of smoking salt was a smart cookie. When wet, salt absorbs flavours really well and, depending on the wood you use, you can achieve an aggressive flavour or a subtle one. Smoked salt gives a great boost to a grilled piece of meat and you can also use it as a straight substitute for normal salt in your rub recipes. Once you have experienced good smoked salt you will find it hard to season meat with anything else!

Smoking salt is a really cool process, but you'll need to use a kettle-type barbecue or a hooded gas one. You'll also need to pre-soak your woodchips in water for an hour.

I love this combination of smoke and rosemary. Rosemary is an oily herb and easy to dry at home. I think you get a better flavour from home-dried herbs, so have a crack at this combination! Just tie fresh rosemary together at the stems and hang it up to dry. It will keep for up to a month if stored in an airtight container.

MAKES 200 G

2 cups coarse rock salt

4 cups hickory or mesquite woodchips

½ cup home-dried rosemary

Wet the salt a little, so it is damp but not slushy.

Prepare your barbecue so you have a small area of indirect heat to one side. If using a gas barbecue, just turn one burner on. Place the salt on the barbecue, away from the heat source.

Add 1 cup of pre-soaked woodchips to the heat source, or smoke box if using gas, and once you have a good smoke going place the lid on the barbecue. Smoke for about 1 hour, adding woodchips as required.

Allow the salt to cool, then mix with the home-dried rosemary.

The salt will keep for 1 month if stored in an airtight container or re-usable grinder.

BREADS
AND BITES

Bread is an integral part of daily life

in most countries around the world. In some cultures it is considered a cornerstone of existence, and it plays a significant role (pardon the pun) in Christian symbolism and ceremony.

Bread is the fork, spoon and plate throughout Central Asia, and it's omnipresent at any Mediterranean table. It is the vehicle that carries and brings flavours together. Where would the burger be without the bun? An Indian meal without the naan?

All great cuisines have a famous bread of some sort and some of them are just perfect for cooking on a barbecue. From a simple damper to more flavourful parathas and focaccias, cooking bread on the barbecue is a great way to experience different styles of breads from around the world.

The trick to cooking bread on the barbecue is understanding the way your barbecue works and how best to control the temperature. This comes with trial and error, just as it does when using an oven. The easiest recipes are the tortillas, parathas and naans, as they are a simple flat-bread style that requires a relatively high heat.

In this chapter you'll find some of the classic breads from different cultures that all do a great barbecue. I've also included a few of my favourite recipes that are suited to being cooked on a barbecue. I've got to admit I'm a sucker for garlic bread every time.

Bruschetta

There is much discussion about what bruschetta really is or isn't. In its purest and simplest form, it is a grilled slice of bread that's simply rubbed with fresh garlic, drizzled with lashings of olive oil and seasoned with salt. A good bruschetta is a celebration of that true culinary champion, extra-virgin olive oil.

The best bread to grill to make bruschetta is sourdough, slightly stale, as traditionally it was a way of using up older bread (the Italians are an economic people!) The bread can then be the vehicle for so many fantastic combinations of toppings.

Bruschetta is great to serve as snacks for a party, in a soup as croutons or under roast meat or stews to soak up the delicious gravy. It can even be turned into quite a substantial meal, depending on the topping.

SERVES 8

12 slices sourdough bread, sliced 2 cm thick

2 garlic cloves, peeled

100 ml best-quality extra-virgin olive oil or more to taste

good-quality crystal or rock salt

Ensure that the barbecue is clean and dry of any oils. Place the slices of bread directly over the heat, allowing them to toast and take on the pattern from the grill. Turn the slices over and repeat the process on the other side.

Remove to a board or large plate and immediately rub the slices of bread once or twice with the peeled cloves of garlic, just to give a hint of garlic aroma.

Liberally drizzle with olive oil and season with salt.

Either enjoy the bruschetta as is or top with anything you desire. You could try using olive bread as a variation.

Marinated fire-roasted pepper with anchovy bruschetta

1 quantity Bruschetta (opposite)
1 quantity Marinated Fire-roasted Peppers with Anchovies (page 80)
Oregano or sweet marjoram leaves to garnish

Top each bruschetta with the peppers and garnish with sweet marjoram
or oregano.

Arrange on platters and serve.

Mozzarella with pepper and basil bruschetta

1 quantity Bruschetta (opposite)
1 quantity Marinated Fire-roasted Peppers with Anchovies (page 80)
1 large buffalo mozzarella, sliced
torn basil leaves to garnish
extra-virgin olive oil
salt
freshly ground black pepper

Top each bruschetta with some roasted peppers and a slice of mozzarella.

Garnish with a few basil leaves, add a drizzle of olive oil and season with salt
and pepper.

Arrange on platters and serve.

Marinated olive and mozzarella bruschetta

1 quantity Bruschetta (opposite)
1 large buffalo mozzarella, sliced
Marinated Olives (page 99)

Top each bruschetta with 2 slices of mozzarella and sprinkle with 1 heaped
tablespoon of the marinated olives.

Arrange on platters and serve.

Simple tomato and garlic bruschetta

1 quantity Bruschetta (page 44)
8 very ripe small tomatoes, halved
chopped basil leaves to garnish
salt
freshly ground black pepper

Squash a tomato over each bruschetta.

Garnish with a few basil leaves and season with salt and pepper.

Arrange on platters and serve.

Fig, mint and mozzarella bruschetta

1 quantity Bruschetta (page 44)
4 ripe figs, sliced
juice of 1 lemon
extra-virgin olive oil
salt
freshly ground black pepper
1 large buffalo mozzarella, sliced
chopped mint leaves to garnish

Only use the ripest figs you can find for this one. Dress the sliced figs with lemon juice, olive oil, salt and pepper.

Top each bruschetta with a layer of dressed figs topped with mozzarella.

Garnish with a little chopped mint and a drizzle of olive oil.

Arrange on platters and serve.

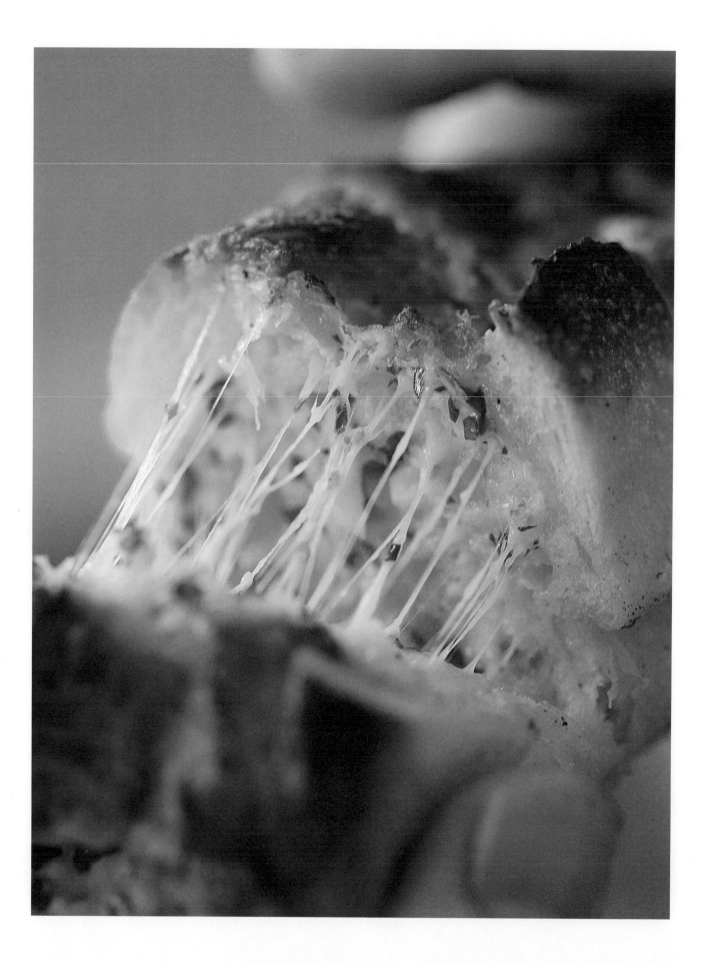

Cheesy garlic bread

Garlic bread is always a winner at a barbecue. It's quick and easy, and hits the spot to help alleviate those hunger pains after you've been struggling to light the barbecue for the last hour. I find it's best to use a baguette, but you could just as easily use a ciabatta.

For me, this recipe is a throwback to Perth in the 1980s, which probably means the '70s everywhere else in terms of cuisine! Garlic bread was huge at the time; every restaurant served it. Making garlic bread was my first job when I was an apprentice chef. The task was approached with great diligence and pride, because if your garlic bread was good, and you sold lots of it, you got the nod from the apprentices who'd come before you. There was also a lot of competition as to who made the best garlic bread. Try my recipe, and you be the judge.

SERVES 4

1 long sourdough baguette

110 g mozzarella ball, chopped

200 g taleggio, chopped

200 g unsalted butter, soft

4 garlic cloves, finely chopped

2 teaspoons chopped flat-leaf parsley

1 teaspoon chopped sweet marjoram

salt

freshly ground black pepper

paprika (your choice of sweet or hot – I prefer sweet)

Use a bread knife to cut diagonal slices along the loaf, cutting only three-quarters of the way into the bread with each slice.

Add the chopped cheeses to the butter, along with the garlic and herbs, and season with salt and pepper.

Spread the mix liberally between each slice of bread. Allow some of the butter to ooze from the top, as this will caramelise while cooking on the barbecue and taste wicked.

Wrap the bread in a doubled-over sheet of foil, leave the top exposed and sprinkle with paprika. Place on the barbecue with the lid on. If you have an uncovered barbecue, completely wrap the bread and just place it on the grill. Cook until crisp.

Serve while hot and the cheese is all gooey and delicious.

Damper

Damper is a true Australian icon of bush cooking and backyard barbecuing. It's a heritage food, its roots going back to the swagmen of our early pioneer days. Usually cooked in the dying embers of an open fire or in a bush oven (a cast-iron pot), it's easily the simplest bread you could make on a barbecue.

The dough is made from the most basic ingredients that a traveller could carry: self-raising flour, lard or butter (more often lard, as it would keep better, and it produces the best results), salt, sugar, milk and water. As a kid, I always made damper when I went camping, but more often than not I was more interested in making it, than eating it – with kids, it's always more about the journey than the destination.

The basic dough can be improved with the addition of herbs, olives or just about anything that takes your fancy. You can even make Damper Doughnuts (page 205), stuffed with marshmallows.

MAKES 1 LOAF

450 g organic self-raising flour

2 teaspoons sugar

1 heaped teaspoon salt

100 g lard or butter

300 ml milk

300 ml water

extra flour for dusting

extra milk for brushing

butter to serve

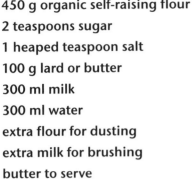

Sieve the flour, sugar and salt together in a bowl.

Using a fork, cut in the lard or butter until you have a texture that resembles breadcrumbs.

Mix in the milk and water, then lightly knead to form a dough.

Pat out onto a well-floured board or tray.

Cut a cross into the dough, brush with milk and lightly flour the top. Place into a foil tray or baking dish.

Prepare your barbecue for indirect cooking on a medium heat (180°C if you have a thermometer). If you are cooking on a gas barbecue with a hood, turn the inner burners off and leave the outer ones on. For coal, build a fire on each side of the barbecue.

Cook the damper until golden or the bread sounds hollow when tapped.

Serve hot with lots of butter.

Focaccia

I think focaccia is an ideal bread to cook on the barbecue, using either a kettle-style model or the hooded variety. The bread is generally not much more than a couple of centimetres thick, as it becomes a little too doughy otherwise. What's great about focaccia is that you can top it with a huge variety of toppings. One suggestion is Marinated Olives (page 99) or chopped rosemary and garlic.

MAKES 1 LOAF

1.5 litres warm water
500 g semolina flour
30 g fresh yeast or 15 g dried yeast
1 tablespoon honey
500 g pasta flour
20 g salt
extra semolina flour for kneading
extra-virgin olive oil
sea salt flakes
freshly ground black pepper
chopped fresh herbs (optional)

Combine the warm water and semolina flour in a large bowl or mixing machine to make a porridge. The mixture should be room temperature.

Add the yeast and honey, using your hands to break up the yeast into the semolina. Allow the mixture to stand for 5–10 minutes, until bubbles start to appear.

Add the flour and salt, working the dough until it is smooth, soft and not too sticky. Dust the dough with a little flour, cover with a moist cloth and leave it to prove until doubled in size. This should take 30–45 minutes.

Tip the dough out onto a clean surface, knock it back and knead again. You may need to dust with a little flour to stop it from sticking.

Roll out the dough into a round, square or oval shape about 2 cm thick. Dust a baking tray with semolina flour, then lay the dough on top and press it out, if need be. Liberally oil the top of the bread and, using your fingertips as if you were playing the piano, press the surface of the bread so that it is pockmarked all over. Season well with salt flakes and a little pepper, and perhaps some fresh herbs and slivers of garlic.

If you are topping the bread with a garnish, simply use the pressing method to push it into the bread, along with a little olive oil.

Allow the focaccia to prove for 40 minutes.

Prepare your barbecue for indirect cooking on a medium–hot heat.

Bake the focaccia until the top is golden and the edges are crispy.

Allow the bread to cool slightly prior to serving. It's best served within 2 hours of baking.

Chapatti

A chapatti is a very simple, firm flour dough that's rolled flat and then cooked on a barbecue hotplate. I like to use my tortilla press when I'm making chapattis – not only is it easy, you also get a great random shape. All you have to do is place a nice portion of dough in the centre of the press and pull down on the handle. Chapattis are best served hot, and they go particularly well with satay skewers or tandoori dishes.

Hands are used more frequently than knives and forks in India, and the chapatti is handy to scoop up all those lovely juices. The addition of a few whole spices like fennel or cumin can make a subtle but great addition to the basic recipe.

MAKES 8–10

1 teaspoon salt
250 g whole wheat atta flour
50 ml sunflower oil

Combine the salt and flour, and add enough water to form a semi-hard dough. Wrap in cling film and rest for 20 minutes.

Divide the dough into 8–10 balls, then either press in a tortilla press or roll out on a clean surface using a rolling pin. You shouldn't need extra flour if the dough is firm enough.

Prepare your barbecue for cooking on a medium heat. Oil the hotplate and cook the chapattis for just a few minutes, turning them often.

Serve hot.

Aloo gobi parathas: roti breads stuffed with cauliflower and potato

My mate Serif's mum comes from India, and she's the best cook. Serif's house was our favourite meeting place when I was growing up: we would hang out in his old man's shed, fixing our bikes trying to get Serif's go-cart to work. His mum always had a huge pot of curry on the stove and we would just help ourselves, but the highlight would be when she had her extended family over. If you were lucky enough to rock around when that was happening you were in for a treat, because that's when parathas were made – awesome roti breads stuffed with meat, vegetables and spices.

These parathas are great by themselves or with a curry, but you don't need to save them for when you're putting on an Indian-themed meal. They should be cooked whenever you have a barbecue! The vegos will love them, especially served with Spiced Yoghurt (page 162) or Spiced Red Bean Salad (page 100).

MAKES 4

ROTI DOUGH

250 g plain flour
pinch of salt
50 ml sunflower oil

FILLING

300 g potatoes
200 g cauliflower
2 tablespoons chopped coriander leaves
2 teaspoons garlic paste
2 teaspoons ginger paste
75 g onion, finely chopped
½ green chilli, chopped
1 teaspoon turmeric
1 teaspoon chilli powder
juice of 1 lime
salt
sunflower oil for frying

To make the dough, combine the flour and salt. Mix in the oil and add enough water to form a soft but not sticky dough. Wrap in cling film and rest for 20 minutes.

Boil the potatoes in their skins in salted water. Meanwhile, in another saucepan, cook the cauliflower in salted water until soft.

Once the potatoes are cooked, peel and mash them. Drain the cauliflower, then crush it and mix it with the potatoes.

Add the remaining ingredients, apart from the salt and oil for frying. When combined, season with salt.

To make the parathas, take a portion of the roti dough and flatten it in your palm. Add a spoonful of the potato and cauliflower mixture, then roll the dough into a ball. Using a rolling pin, flatten the ball to around 1 cm thick.

Prepare your barbecue for cooking on a medium heat. Lightly oil the hotplate and cook the parathas until both sides are golden and cooked through.

Serve straightaway.

Naan

You'll find this type of bread across the whole of Asia. The most famous variety is the Indian incarnation, cooked in the terracotta tandoor ovens of the Punjab. Naans are simple to make, and they are a great alternative to serving everyday breads at a barbecue. They come either plain or packed with a variety of fillings like dried fruit and coconut.

You could add chopped garlic to the clarified butter in this recipe if you'd like a more flavoursome naan. This bread is ideal to serve with Pumpkin Biryani (page 86) or Barbecued Pepper Chicken Curry (page 173).

MAKES 6

525 g whole wheat atta flour or strong plain flour

pinch of salt

10 g fresh yeast or 5 g dried yeast

1 teaspoon caster sugar

125 ml warm water

1 medium egg, beaten

3 tablespoons biodynamic yoghurt

extra flour

clarified butter to serve

Combine the flour and salt, and mix well.

Mix the yeast and sugar with the warm water and allow to stand for 5–10 minutes, until the mixture starts to foam. Add the egg and yoghurt.

Combine the yeast mixture with the flour and knead until you have a smooth, soft dough. Cover with a wet cloth, place in a warm place and leave it to prove until doubled in size.

Once the dough has proved, knock it back and allow it to prove again until it has doubled in size once again.

Divide the dough into equal-sized balls. Pat them out on a floured surface to a roughly round or oval shape, the thickness of half a centimetre. Do not roll them out with a rolling pin.

Cook the naan straight on the grill racks of a medium–hot kettle barbecue with the lid on. You could also cook them directly on a dry hotplate with the hood down.

Brush the cooked naan with clarified butter and serve while hot.

Polenta

The Spanish brought corn to Europe from the New World, and it is now a staple of many cuisines. I particularly love the way the Italians have embraced it. When I worked at London's River Café we served polenta every year, from late autumn into winter, while corn was in season. It's important to use a good-quality, ground polenta; I find the coarser, bramata style is best. Try to avoid the quick-cook stuff – it just doesn't have the flavour of the coarse, slow-cooking polenta.

The best part about cooking polenta is the fantastic crust at the bottom of the pan. We used to fight over the crust and add butter, parmesan and chopped chilli to it at the end. Gary, one of the Aussie chefs I worked with at the River Café, put me onto that little indulgence.

You will need to prepare the polenta in advance, as it has to set and then cool completely before it can be sliced and barbecued. Polenta can be served as a substitute for bread and it's also fantastic to give to your vegan mates to fill them up! It's a great accompaniment to grilled meats, especially pork, lamb or a great steak. Try the toppings I've suggested here, or simply top it with grilled field mushrooms and cheese.

SERVES 8

1.75 litres water

salt

300 g polenta

100 g unsalted butter

200 g parmesan, finely grated

freshly ground black pepper

Bring the water to the boil in a heavy-bottomed saucepan. Season well with salt.

Lower the heat to a simmer and slowly add the polenta in a continuous stream, stirring with a whisk until completely incorporated.

Bring the polenta to the boil. It should take on a thick quality, like slowly bubbling lava. Turn the heat down to low, so it bubbles only every so often, and cook for 30–40 minutes, until the grains are only just soft. Stir from time to time, to prevent the polenta from catching.

When cooked, stir in the butter, parmesan and pepper. Pour onto a wooden board or large plate and allow to set.

When completely cool, cut the polenta into strips or wedges and barbecue on a grill rack until crisp.

Coppa di Parma and blue cheese

Serve this polenta with a simple rocket salad.

100 g gorgonzola dolce
1 tablespoon mascarpone
1 teaspoon chopped sweet marjoram or oregano leaves
Coppa di Parma or prosciutto, sliced
1 quantity Polenta (page 60), grilled
juice of ½ lemon
extra-virgin olive oil

Place the gorgonzola, mascarpone and marjoram or oregano in a small saucepan, and slowly cook until the cheese is just melted.

Place slices of Coppa di Parma on the grilled polenta, then dress with the cheese sauce, a squeeze of lemon juice and a drizzle of good olive oil.

Butter, chilli and cheese

This one's an old favourite amongst chefs. There are no measurements – just use your intuition!

1 quantity Polenta (page 60), grilled
unsalted butter, soft
parmesan, grated
red chillies, chopped

Simply spread the grilled polenta with butter (chefs tend to think the more butter, the better the taste), sprinkle with cheese and top with chopped chillies.

Quesadillas

Quesadillas are the ultimate fast food. Ideally, you should use raw dough to make them, although you can cheat and use flour tortillas from the supermarket and stuff them with your filling of choice. The great thing about making your own dough is that you can flavour it with chillies, cheese or fresh herbs.

Quesadillas are perfect for stuffing with Refried Beans (page 93).

MAKES 10–12

300 g masa harina (tortilla flour)
50 g plain flour
½ teaspoon baking powder
3 tablespoons corn oil or
  vegetable oil
1 large egg, beaten
175 ml milk

Place the dry ingredients in a large bowl and combine thoroughly.

Stir in the oil, egg and enough milk to make a firm dough.

Form into balls and press out into large circles.

Place your filling in the middle of one half of each quesadilla, then fold over. Seal the edges by pressing them together, wetting the edges slightly if necessary to get them to stick.

Prepare your barbecue for cooking on a medium heat. Lightly oil the hotplate of your barbecue or griddle pan and cook the quesadillas for 2–3 minutes on each side.

Zucchini and cheese quesadillas

1 zucchini, grated
1 cup grated cheddar
1 cup grated mozzarella
2 tablespoons chopped basil leaves
salt
freshly ground black pepper
1 quantity Quesadilla dough (see above)

Combine the grated zucchini and cheeses. Add the basil, salt and pepper. Place the cheese mix inside the quesadillas and seal.

Cook as described above.

Cheese quesadillas

½ cup grated cheddar
½ cup grated mozzarella
¼ cup grated parmesan
100 g gorgonzola dolce or taleggio
salt
freshly ground black pepper
1 quantity Quesadilla dough (see above)

Combine the cheeses with a little salt and pepper. Place inside the quesadillas and seal.

Cook as described above.

Tortillas

Tortilla means 'little cake' in Spanish, and is not to be confused with the Spanish omelette of the same name. Tortillas are generally made using a ground corn flour called masa harina, which means 'dough flour'.

Tortillas are fundamental to Mexican cuisine, forming the basis of many dishes. They are also easy to make and very economical. All you need is a tortilla press, and off you go! Get them mastered and you can be making tacos, tostadas and chilaquiles. You can use a number of recipes in this book to fill the very versatile tortilla. Try the Suckling Pig Tortillas (page 186) or your could even use the marinated skirt steak (see the Aussie Steak Sandwich for example, page 144).

MAKES 6–8

275 g masa harina (tortilla flour)
½ teaspoon salt
300 ml water, lukewarm
    temperature

Combine the masa harina and salt in a large bowl.

Add 250 ml of the water and mix until it forms a dough. Test the dough in your press by placing a small ball of dough between 2 sheets of plastic bag and closing the press. If the dough is too dry, it will crumble; if it is too wet, it will stick to the plastic.

If the dough is too wet, add more masa; if it's too dry, add a little water. It's hard to say how much water will be required as humidity affects the dough, as does the age of the flour. Fresh masa needs less water than older flour.

If the dough is correct, form balls about 4 cm in diameter. Place the balls, one at a time, between 2 sheets of plastic bag and press to flatten into a circle about 10 cm wide. Remove the top plastic sheet, then lift and turn the tortilla over onto your palm and peel away the other sheet of plastic.

Prepare your barbecue for cooking on a medium heat. Place the tortillas on the grill top, or on a heavy skillet if using a kettle or open coal fire. Cook for 1 minute, until the edges curl upwards, then flip and cook for another minute. The tortillas should be lightly speckled; the first side cooked is the top.

Eat the tortillas straightaway, or keep them warm by wrapping them in a cloth and placing them inside a heavy warm pot.

VEGETABLES AND SALADS

In many people's minds, a barbecue is a totally meat-oriented feast. Most self-respecting grill jockeys flex their culinary muscles with their carnivorous exploits, but there is nothing I like more than a good selection of vegetable and salad offerings to go with my grilled protein. It's also the perfect test of one's skill on the grill, your control of the coal!

My vegan and vegetarian friends appreciate my efforts to include them when an invitation to a barbecue goes out. Vegetables can be as easy or as complicated as you want them to be. You can stuff them with wonderful aromatic spices or fresh fragrant herbs. Thinly slice grilled vegetables and give them a simple dressing, or serve them whole cooked on the coals. Salads can be put together in a flash and some dishes such as Korean kimchi aren't even cooked – they are pickled and served as the perfect accompaniment to spicy barbecued meats. The key is to use fresh ingredients to get the best flavours possible.

So, meat-eaters and vegos alike, get stuck in!

Grilled verdure misté

So, you've gone all out with your pit of fire, and you've slow-cooked your pork shoulder or hunk of beef. It's an orgy of carnivorous delights and now your mates have turned up, and, surprise, surprise, one of them has brought a vegan! No drama you say, and really there shouldn't be, not when you can impress everyone with this great combination of barbecued vegies.

It's hard to give exact volumes for this recipe, as it's more or less of what you like, but the general process is what is important. Firstly, build your fire or adjust your gas so that you have a hot side and a cooler side of the barbecue. Secondly, always start with the vegetables that will take the longest to cook. Adding a spray of water to the vegetables while they're cooking speeds the process along, as the water evaporates on the barbecue, creating steam. I never add oil because it burns by the time the vegies are cooked, giving them an unpleasant taste.

Serve garnished with freshly cut herbs or maybe some balsamic vinegar or feta.

SERVES 4

pumpkin (butternut, squash,
    crown prince), peeled

salt

freshly ground black pepper

baby leeks

fennel

red onions

finger eggplant

zucchini

kipfler potatoes

DRESSING

2 garlic cloves, peeled

salt

2 tablespoons chopped herbs
    (basil, marjoram or dried wild
    oregano)

2 tablespoons white wine vinegar

3 tablespoons extra-virgin olive oil

freshly ground black pepper

If you are using butternut pumpkin, cut in half and then into wedges about as thick as your finger. If you are using a round pumpkin, cut into crescents, again about as thick as your finger. Toss the pumpkin with a little water and salt and pepper.

Cut the other vegetables into pieces that are sympathetic to their natural shapes, relative to their size and the other vegetables you are cooking. Toss with a little water and salt and pepper.

Place the vegetables on the hottest part of the barbecue to char them with the marks of the grill, then move them to the lower heat. Cook until just tender, as the residual heat will continue to steam and soften the vegetables once they are removed from the heat.

Transfer the vegetables to a large bowl as they cook, taking care to mix the different varieties together.

To make the dressing, place the garlic in a mortar and pound with a little salt and the fresh herbs to form a paste. Add white wine vinegar and olive oil to make a vinaigrette, then toss with the grilled vegetables.

Season with salt and pepper, then serve.

Robatayaki vegetables

Robatayaki is a style of cooking seafood and vegetables, and less frequently meat and poultry, over a charcoal grill. Traditionally, robatayakis were inns or meeting places that had an open fire (robata) in the middle of the room, the centre of activity. As with Japanese food in general, presentation is of major importance, so most robatayaki dishes are small morsels and are simply presented on bamboo skewers. Common ingredients include asparagus, mushrooms, tofu and finger eggplants. They're generally seasoned with kecap manis or miso sauce.

Asparagus

SERVES 4

24 thick asparagus spears
kecap manis
1 teaspoon sesame seeds

Soak 8 bamboo skewers for 1 hour in some water.

Trim the asparagus to 12 cm lengths, making sure they are perfectly even and the base of each stem is cut on a slight angle.

Thread 3 pieces of asparagus onto a skewer. Make sure they're evenly spaced and threaded halfway along the asparagus. Repeat with the remaining asparagus, allowing 2 skewers per person.

Place on the grill and cook for 2 minutes on each side.

Remove to a plate, drizzle with kecap manis and sprinkle with a few sesame seeds. Serve with asian herbs.

Miso eggplant

SERVES 6

12 finger eggplants, halved lengthwise
100 g Miso Marinade (page 23)

Soak 12 bamboo skewers for 1 hour in some water.

Carefully cut a crisscross pattern into the flesh of the eggplants. Thread 2 eggplant halves onto each skewer. Repeat with the remaining eggplants, allowing 2 skewers per person.

Brush the eggplants with half the marinade and allow to infuse for 20 minutes.

Place the eggplants flesh side down on a hot grill for 1–2 minutes. Turn them over and cook for a further 5 minutes, or until soft.

Remove the eggplants to plates and brush with a little more miso marinade.

Baba ganoush

Eggplants are perfect for cooking on the barbecue, either grilled or charred in the fire. For this recipe, they are cooked whole until they are soft and take on an incredible smoky flavour. Baba ganoush is great as a dip to share while the main meal is cooking, or as an accompaniment with kofte, shish or simply grilled lamb, chicken, salmon or mackerel.

SERVES 4

2 large eggplants
salt
freshly ground black pepper
1 large tablespoon tahini
2 garlic cloves, chopped
juice of 2 lemons
2 tablespoons olive oil
1 teaspoon toasted cumin seeds
to serve

Place the eggplants directly in the fire or on the grill and allow to cook until very soft and charred all over. They will look burnt. Remove from the fire and allow to cool.

Peel away the burnt outer skin with a small, sharp knife or cut in half and scoop out the flesh. Place the flesh in a sieve or colander to drain, as the eggplants will have a lot of moisture in them.

Using a whisk, fork or blender, break down the eggplant to a pulp.

Season with salt and pepper, then add tahini and chopped garlic. Add the lemon juice and olive oil, and combine.

Check the seasoning and texture. The baba ganoush should be creamy.

Serve sprinkle with toasted cumin seeds.

Grilled haloumi

I've only been to one Greek island, Mykonos, but I've been to many good Greek restaurants in Sydney, London and Melbourne, which has the third-largest Greek population outside Greece. But the best Greek experience I've ever had was when I was in Wellington, New Zealand. We went to the house of a Greek Cypriot family who put on a barbecue like nothing you have ever seen. Their son was a cheese-maker whose speciality was an authentic Cypriot haloumi cheese flecked with fresh mint, a traditional addition.

There is only one way to eat haloumi, and that is simply grilled on a hotplate and served with fresh lemon and mint. It's a great way to get the hordes' appetites started and kept at bay while you get on with the main show.

SERVES 6

200 g good-quality haloumi (Greek if possible)
1 tablespoon olive oil
2 tablespoons chopped mint leaves
juice of 1 lemon

Prepare your barbecue for cooking over a medium–high heat.

Cut the haloumi into flattish rectangles, about a finger thick.

Pour the oil onto the hot griddle or barbecue hotplate. Cook the haloumi until golden and crispy on both sides.

Remove to a plate and scatter with chopped mint leaves and a squeeze of lemon juice.

Serve hot.

Coal-baked artichokes

I love artichokes and the endless ways of preparing them. The method I saw demonstrated when I attended a cooking school in a small Sicilian village called Regaleali is truly the best and most simple.

A fire in a large open pit is allowed to burn down to a mass of smouldering coals, into which whole artichokes are pushed. It means that you don't end up with bitter, stained fingers from cleaning the artichokes first. Once they are cooked, you can do what you like with them – preserve them in oil, make salads with them or serve them in the dressing described here.

There are many varieties of artichokes, but I recommend that you use the larger globe or smaller violet or spiny ones. Choose artichokes that are firm and have a tightly closed flower, as these will have a smaller percentage of the furry choke at the centre.

SERVES 4

4 large globe artichokes or 8 violet or spiny artichokes

Build a good hot coal base and allow it to burn down to an even white bed of ashen coals. The coals should be deep enough to cover three-quarters of each artichoke.

Cut the stem of each artichoke to about 2 cm from the base. Use a serrated knife to trim the top by around 2 cm.

Push the artichokes into the coals using a long pair of tongs, to avoid burning yourself. Place the artichokes as close together as possible and push the coals up and around them.

Allow the artichokes to cook until they are tender to the prick of a knife or skewer.

Remove to a large bowl and allow them to cool so you can handle them.

Once cool, use a small knife to peel off the outer leaves, one at a time, until you reach the first of the tender inside leaves. Trim the stem by scraping it with the knife. Cut the artichokes in half and remove all the furry choke fibres.

Artichokes with lemon, honey, thyme and almond dressing

 We used to cook this recipe at the River Café in London, and it's a great combination. Make sure you use a good-quality honey.

SERVES 4

1 quantity Coal-baked Artichokes
  (see page 76)
1 garlic clove, peeled
1 tablespoon thyme leaves
salt
1 tablespoon honey
zest and juice of 1 lemon
100 ml olive oil
freshly cracked black pepper
½ cup toasted, flaked almonds
  to serve

While you are waiting for the artichokes to cool, pound the garlic, thyme and a little salt in a mortar to a paste.

Add the honey and lemon juice and zest, and combine well. Mix in the olive oil.

Peel and cut the artichokes into quarters. While they are still warm, toss with the dressing and season with salt and pepper to taste.

Serve sprinkled with almonds.

Fire-roasted peppers

Just about every Italian I have spoken to about barbecuing capsicums or peppers says that putting them directly into the fire to cook gives them a flavour that's so sublime, no gas grill can match it. This method is great, as the direct contact with the coals speeds the process along.

I once worked with the Sicilian director Carmelo Musca. Gesticulating passionately, he described the way his mother prepared sweet peppers. With my imagination stimulated, I could smell the sweet, burnt skin blistering to reveal the lush flesh impregnated with the soul of the fire.

These peppers work a treat on Bruschetta (page 44). It's best to use long, pointed peppers. The great thing about using a plastic bag when preparing them is that you can leave all the charred and discarded material inside the bag, which you can then tie up and dispose of without any mess!

SERVES 6

6 firm-fleshed peppers

Build a good hot coal base and allow it to burn down to an even white bed of ashen coals.

Place the peppers around the edge of the fire, and use long-handled tongs to turn them so their skin is charred evenly on all sides. When the peppers are blackened all over, either put them in a stainless-steel bowl and cover with cling wrap or put them in a plastic bag and tie to seal. Allow the peppers to cool sufficiently so you can handle them.

Prepare the peppers by pushing the charred skin away from the flesh, removing the stalk and slitting the peppers to remove the seeds.

Marinated fire-roasted peppers with anchovies

salt

freshly ground black pepper

extra-virgin olive oil

2 teaspoons chopped sweet marjoram or basil

1 quantity Fire-roasted Peppers (see above)

12 anchovy fillets

1 garlic clove, sliced

Sprinkle a plate with salt and pepper, a little olive oil and half the herbs. Place the peppers on the platter.

Arrange the anchovies, remaining herbs and sliced garlic over the top of the peppers.

To serve, season with pepper and drizzle once again with olive oil.

Baked sweet potatoes

Sweet potatoes or kumara have been cultivated as a source of food for thousands of years. New Zealand's Maori have a long history of cultivating kumara, though compared to the varieties we eat today they tended to be small – generally no bigger than a finger. The sweet potato evolved from an American vegetable, and over time red, gold and orange potatoes have been cultivated. It's a very nutritious vegetable, high in vitamins A and C.

There are endless ways to prepare sweet potatoes, but, just like potatoes baked in their skins, you can't beat the flavour when they're simply prepared. Here are two of my favourite ways to cook sweet potatoes on the barbecue.

Baked sweet potatoes with green chilli and lemon oil

SERVES 4

4 sweet potatoes, washed and dried

2 green chillies, seeded and finely chopped

zest of 1 lemon

2 tablespoons extra-virgin olive oil

salt

Firmly wrap each sweet potato in 2 sheets of foil.

Prepare your barbecue for cooking over a medium heat. If using charcoal, insert the sweet potatoes along the edge of the coals, leaving room for the main event; if using gas, place them over the gas burners on the grilling bars.

Cook the sweet potatoes until they are quite soft. The cooking time will depend on the size of the vegetables, and may take about 30 minutes.

When cooked, discard the foil, slit the potatoes open with a sharp knife and place on a serving plate.

Combine the chopped chillies with the lemon zest and olive oil.

To serve, dress the sweet potatoes with the chillies and season with salt.

Baked sweet potatoes with speck, cloves and maple syrup

SERVES 4

4 sweet potatoes, washed and
　dried

8 strips of speck or smoked streaky
　bacon

4 cloves

2 tablespoons maple syrup

salt

freshly cracked black pepper

Wrap each sweet potato in 2 pieces of speck or smoked streaky bacon. Use cloves to secure the bacon.

Firmly wrap each sweet potato in 2 sheets of foil.

Prepare your barbecue for cooking over a medium heat. If using charcoal, insert the sweet potatoes along the edge of the coals; if using gas, place them over the gas burners on the grilling bars.

Cook the sweet potatoes until they are quite soft. Depending on the size of the vegetables, this may take 30 minutes.

When cooked, discard the foil, slit the potatoes open with a sharp knife and place on a serving plate.

Drizzle the potatoes with maple syrup and season with salt and pepper. Serve straightaway.

Stuffed gem squash

I first encountered gem squash when I was travelling and surfing my way around South Africa. I pretty much had them with every meal. They were sometimes referred to as cricket ball squash, as they resemble a cricket ball in size. Whenever there was a *braai* (barbecue) happening at whatever backpackers I was staying at, the squash would be stabbed with a knife and put on coals to roast. When they were cooked, the top would be cut off, the seeds scooped out and a knob of butter placed inside, along with a little salt and pepper.

Later, when I was at the River Café, we served them as antipasti, stuffed with olives and sun-dried tomatoes, which certainly added a different dimension. As an alternative you could use spaghetti squash, small onion squash or pumpkins.

SERVES 6

6 fist-sized gem squash, washed

½ quantity Marinated Olives (page 99)

6 semi sun-dried tomatoes

100 g feta, cubed

Prepare your barbecue for cooking over a medium heat.

Prick each squash with a metal skewer, inserted from the top into the centre. Place the squash around the coals, or directly over the heat of a gas barbecue, and cook until tender.

When cooked and cooled a little, use a serrated knife to cut the top off each squash, cutting about a quarter of the way down. Scoop out the seeds, and reserve the tops to use as lids.

Combine the marinated olives with the tomatoes and feta, and divide between the squash, filling right to the top. Place the lids on top and serve.

Shaved fennel and celery salad

I can't remember exactly when I fell in love with fennel, but I know it was since I left Australia to go travelling. It was probably when I first experienced a Florentine fennel *finnochio* – those plump, round, firm, crisp and bulbous fennels from Italy.

I love the fresh aniseed flavour of fennel, and it is an excellent digestive. I find that a fennel salad is the perfect antidote to rich barbecued meats. You can slice or shave fennel, or cut it into largish wedges to munch on.

This recipe is so simple and fresh, you'll keep making it whether you're having a barbecue or not. It also uses the pale inside leaves of celery.

SERVES 4

2 large bulbs firm round fennel
1 cup pale celery leaves and stems
2 tablespoons biodynamic yoghurt
1 tablespoon lemon juice
1 tablespoon extra-virgin olive oil
pinch of salt

Wash the fennel in cold water and remove any brown outer fronds. Pick the herb tops from the fennel and reserve for the salad. Wash the celery leaves and stems.

Cut the fennel in half lengthwise and finely slice, cutting across the rings of the bulb. Finely chop the celery and fennel tops then toss together.

Combine the yoghurt with the lemon juice and olive oil and season with salt.

Dress the fennel and celery with the yoghurt dressing and serve.

Whole pumpkin biryani

The first time I ate a whole stuffed pumpkin was when I was staying in Plettenbergbaai in South Africa, a place that reminded me of Byron Bay. While I was there I had the most amazing *braai* (barbecue) I have ever experienced.

For this recipe I have taken another influence, Indian, which is strong in South Africa, and combined it with pumpkin. Vegetable biryanis are more common than meat ones so it makes sense really. It takes a little preparation, but if you're going on a picnic you could prepare this and wrap it up to take along, as it travels so well.

SERVES 8

100 g basmati rice

1 large butternut pumpkin (1.5–2 kg)

2 tablespoons canned chopped tomatoes

1 tablespoon chopped mint leaves

1 tablespoon coriander leaves

pinch of fresh saffron

1 teaspoon garam masala to serve

MARINADE

10 g garlic, peeled

10 g ginger, peeled

2 red chillies

sunflower oil

4 tablespoons yoghurt

juice of 1 lemon

1 teaspoon ground turmeric

salt to taste

SPICE MIX

2 tablespoons vegetable oil

1 onion, sliced

3 cardamom pods, crushed

¼ teaspoon ground cinnamon

2 cloves

1 bay leaf

Wash and drain the rice until the water runs clear, then boil until two-thirds cooked. Drain and refresh.

To make the marinade, purée the garlic, ginger and chillies with a little sunflower oil to help loosen the mix. Combine with the remaining marinade ingredients.

Halve the butternut pumpkin, remove the seeds and scoop out the flesh to create a large cavity in each half. Chop the scooped-out pumpkin into dice and add half the dice to the marinade. Keep the remaining pumpkin dice for soup or another use.

To make the spice mix, heat the oil in a heavy-bottomed frying pan or on the hotplate and cook the onion. Add the remaining spice mix ingredients, and fry until slightly golden. Remove from the heat and set aside.

Combine the marinated pumpkin with the canned tomatoes.

Spoon the pumpkin mixture into the 2 pumpkin halves, then add alternate layers of cooked rice, spice mix, chopped mint and coriander leaves.

Sprinkle saffron over the top of each pumpkin half then sandwich the 2 halves together. Wrap tightly in 3–4 layers of foil and place in the coals or on the edge of the barbecue to cook for 1½ hours.

To serve, open the 2 halves and sprinkle over garam masala.

Barbecued corn with bacon and chilli butter

Corn on the cob is one of those things that's enjoyed by the whole family. I love that it's such a simple thing to cook and that eating it is so hands-on. If you prefer not to use chilli in the butter, use parmesan or anything you fancy.

I've often come across corn recipes like this one while researching American barbecuing techniques. Here, I have combined the flavours with a barbecued corn dish I had in New York at a funky Cuban diner. The highlight that day was not the corn but that I saw Meg White from the White Stripes there having lunch. The lime chilli butter they served with the corn was great though.

SERVES 4

4 corn cobs, in their husks
8 rashers smoked streaky bacon
freshly ground black pepper

CHILLI BUTTER
100 g softened unsalted butter
1 red chilli, chopped
zest of 1 lime
salt
freshly ground black pepper

Prepare your barbecue for cooking over a medium heat.

Prepare the corn by pulling back the outer husks and removing all the strands of fibre, but without removing the husks.

Place 2 strips of streaky bacon on either side of each cob and season with pepper. Wrap the corn cobs back in their husks and secure with string at the top and bottom.

Cook the corn cobs for 30 minutes, continually turning them to prevent the husks from burning.

Meanwhile, make the chilli butter by combining the butter, chilli and lime zest, and seasoning with salt and pepper.

When the corn is cooked, remove to a serving dish, untie the string and peel back the husk. Serve with a dollop of chilli butter.

Balsamic rosemary onions

A barbecue just doesn't feel like a barbecue unless there are onions. This recipe is a great way to serve them as an accompaniment to whole joints of beef or lamb cooked on the barbecue. I like to use a charcoal fire for this one – which isn't to say that cooking the onions over gas won't be as awesome! Make sure the onions you choose have firm, intact and clean skins.

The flavours in this recipe are akin to sweet and sour: you have the wonderful sweetness of the slow-cooked onion, and the woody, sweet and sharp flavour of the balsamic. Try cooking them in a conventional oven as well, I would recommend cooking them for 45 minutes at about 160°C.

SERVES 6

6 medium brown onions
120 ml balsamic vinegar
salt
freshly ground black pepper
300 g butter, cut into 12 cubes
6 sprigs rosemary

Prepare your barbecue for cooking over a medium heat.

Cut a deep cross into the top of each onion, cutting one-third of the way into the vegetable.

Force your thumb into the incision and prise it open a little. Place 1–2 teaspoons of balsamic vinegar inside, then season with salt and pepper. Press a cube of butter into each onion, followed by a sprig of rosemary.

Arrange 3 squares of foil per onion. Place the onion in the centre of the layers of foil, bring the edges up and together over the top of the onion and twist lightly together.

Place around the edges of your charcoal fire or over the direct heat of a gas grill. Cook for 30–40 minutes, until the onions are tender to the prick of a small sharp knife.

Remove from the fire and carefully untwist the foil. Gently prise open the onions and divide the remaining butter and balsamic between them. Taste with your fingers and correct the seasoning.

Rewrap the onions and allow them to cook for a further 10 minutes.

Once cooked, remove the onions from the heat and allow them to stand for a few minutes. Remove from the foil and transfer to a serving plate.

To serve, gently squeeze the bottom of the onions as you would a baked potato, so they open a little.

Caribbean rice and peas

••••••   This classic Caribbean dish is perfect served with the hot, aromatic flavours of Jerked Chicken (page 168–9) or Jerked Red Fish (page 125). It's sometimes known as Dirty Rice, probably because of the effect of the beans on the rice, but in no way does it reflect its wonderful flavour.

It's an easy dish to prepare and can be cooked outside on the side burner of the barbecue or indoors on the stove.

SERVES 4

225 g can black-eye beans

700 ml water

400 ml can coconut cream

1 teaspoon chopped thyme leaves

1 teaspoon Scotch bonnet chilli (or other hot red chilli), seeded and chopped

2 spring onions, chopped

salt

freshly ground black pepper

450 g basmati rice, washed 3 times

25 g butter

¼ cup chopped coriander leaves and spring onions to serve

Place the beans, water, coconut cream, thyme, chilli and spring onions in a saucepan, and season to taste. Bring to the boil.

Add the washed rice and butter, and boil for 2–3 minutes. Lower the heat to a simmer, cover with a lid and cook for 35 minutes.

Once cooked, stir and serve.

Baked beans

Legumes such as borlotti, cannellini and kidney beans are a fantastic accompaniment to a barbecue. Fresh legumes are generally available during spring and early summer, which means they are at their best when you want to crank up the barbecue. You can also use dried beans, which you can buy at most supermarkets. If you like your beans to have a smoky flavour, try using a chipotle (a dried smoked jalapeño) instead of a dried chilli. Any leftovers can be used to make Refried Beans (page 93) for an accompaniment to Mexican-style dishes.

I like to use Qbags (see page 6, Equipment & Tips) to cook the beans, as there is less messing about, but if you don't have them you can use an enamel or metal roasting dish instead.

SERVES 8

250 g dried or 500 g freshly podded cannellini or borlotti beans

1 teaspoon bicarbonate of soda (if using dried beans)

400 g can chopped or puréed Roma tomatoes

1 sprig rosemary

small bunch sage

2 celery stalks

5 garlic cloves, peeled

1 dried chilli or chipotle chilli

salt

freshly ground black pepper

extra-virgin olive oil

juice of 1 lemon

If you're using dried beans, soak them overnight in plenty of cold water and add 1 teaspoon of bicarbonate of soda (this helps to soften the skins). If you're using fresh beans, just wash and drain them.

Prepare your barbecue for cooking over a medium heat.

Combine the beans and tomatoes in a bowl. Transfer to a roasting dish or Qbags.

Sandwich the rosemary and sage between the 2 celery stalks and tie together to prevent the herbs from mixing in with the beans when cooking. Put this in with the beans, along with the garlic and chilli. Top with water (250 ml if using fresh beans, 500 ml if using dried).

Either seal the bags with 2 firm folds or wrap the dish with foil and seal well.

Place on the barbecue hotplate and cook for 40 minutes, until the beans are soft and most of the liquid has been absorbed.

When cooked, open the bags or remove the foil and discard the celery and herbs and dried chilli. Stir the beans and mash a few with the back of a spoon.

Transfer to a serving bowl, season with salt and pepper, and finish with a splash of extra-virgin olive oil and lemon juice.

Refried beans

The original name for these beans, *frijoles refrito*, doesn't mean that the beans are fried twice. They're simply baked or boiled and then fried with lard or oil. Lard is the better of the two because of its richer flavour, but for those with an aversion to lard, olive oil is fine. I generally use the leftovers from my Baked Beans (page 92). It's important that the beans are relatively free of liquid.

Refried beans are great with Tortillas (page 65) or Quesadillas (page 64), or as a dip served with tortilla chips. They can also accompany grilled meat or chicken. Think of this dish as Mexican mash!

SERVES 4

100 g lard or 100 ml olive oil

½ quantity Baked Beans (opposite)

100 g grated cheddar to serve

salt

freshly ground black pepper

Prepare your barbecue for cooking over a medium heat.

Heat some lard or oil on the barbecue hotplate and add a couple of large spoonfuls of beans. Mash with a scraper and repeat the process until all the beans are cooked, adding a little lard or oil as you go.

Shape the mash into a sausage and remove to a serving dish.

To serve, sprinkle with grated cheese and season with salt and pepper.

Rustic Spanish potatoes

Potatoes have been a staple part of Western diets for centuries, thanks to the Spanish bringing them to Europe along with their plunder from the Americas. The potato took a while to take off, as it was seen as a food for the underclasses, and also because of its association with poison, as it is a member of the deadly nightshade family.

Because we owe it to the Spanish for spuds, I thought I'd include a rustic Spanish-style potato dish. It's great with meat and fish, and is served warm. I use Qbags (see page 6, Equipment & Tips) to do mine on the barbecue, but you could also use a saucepan.

SERVES 6

500 g new potatoes, washed

2 garlic cloves, chopped

12 vine-ripened cherry tomatoes, crushed

1 red pepper, cut into large dice

salt

freshly ground black pepper

100 ml olive oil

175 ml white wine

pinch of saffron

1 tablespoon chopped flat-leaf parsley to serve

Prepare your barbecue for cooking over a medium heat.

Cut the potatoes so they are all an equal size.

If you are using a saucepan, place the potatoes and garlic in a bowl. Put the tomatoes and red pepper in a separate bowl and season with salt and pepper. Heat the oil, then add the potatoes and garlic and cook until the outer edges begin to go translucent. Add the tomatoes and red pepper, and fry for 1 minute. Add the wine and saffron, and allow to gently simmer for 40 minutes, until the potatoes are tender, the tomatoes have broken down and the peppers are soft. When cooked, remove from the heat and allow to stand.

If you are using a Qbag, combine the ingredients in a bowl and season with salt and pepper. Place the mixture in the bag (or bags), seal and place on the barbecue to cook for about 40 minutes. Shake the bag from time to time. When cooked, remove from the heat and allow to stand.

Check the seasoning and serve the potatoes topped with chopped parsley.

Grilled tomatoes and cottage cheese

 You can't have a barbecue without tomatoes showing up in some form or other, whether in a straight salad or in tasty sauces and glazes.

The big trend nowadays is for 'heirloom' varieties, the types of tomatoes that used to be grown but which for commercial reasons have dropped by the wayside – whether because of the small volumes they produced or because they don't travel well to market.

When we filmed an episode of *Surfing the Menu* on the Mornington Peninsula in Victoria, we visited a garden called Heronswood that specialises in growing and sourcing heirloom plants. You can buy an amazing number of tomato varieties online (www.diggers.com.au) and it's worth having a go, because there is nothing like the flavour of home-grown tomatoes.

My granddad always said that you can't beat an English tomato, and this recipe is inspired by the wonderful tomatoes I get from the Isle of Wight. Serve this dish with spicy Peri-Peri Chicken(page 172).

SERVES 6

1 kg mixed variety tomatoes, washed

salt

3 tablespoons extra-virgin olive oil

1 tablespoon chopped rosemary leaves

250 g tub cottage cheese

1 garlic clove, chopped

freshly cracked black pepper

fresh herbs (flat-leaf parsley, mint, oregano, etc.), chopped

Prepare your barbecue for cooking over a high heat.

Cut the tomatoes in half, in irregular shapes. Season with a little salt, pour on a little olive oil and add the rosemary.

Combine the cottage cheese with the remaining olive oil, garlic, salt, pepper and half the chopped soft herbs.

Place the tomatoes cut side down on a very hot barbecue grill and cook until charred.

When cooked, remove to a serving plate. Scatter over the cottage cheese mixture and season.

To serve, garnish with the remaining fresh herbs.

Panzanella

This traditional Tuscan salad is served in summer when tomatoes are at their ripest and basil is at its most aromatic. These top-quality ingredients are bound with fantastic extra-virgin olive oil, for, like most great salads, panzanella is only equal to the sum of its parts.

I love panzanella, as it goes so well with everything: you can serve it with seafood such as prawns, lobster and squid; with meat, either chicken or lamb; or as a stand-alone salad. I like to use overripe tomatoes, as they are juiciest. If you like, to finish you could add some Marinated Fire-roasted Peppers (page 80), half a dozen anchovies and some fresh buffalo mozzarella.

SERVES 6

½ quantity Bruschetta (page 44)

500 g overripe vine-ripened tomatoes

1 small bunch basil leaves, picked

2 garlic cloves, peeled

salt

2 tablespoons red wine vinegar

100 ml best-quality extra-virgin olive oil

freshly ground black pepper

handful wide-leaf rocket

Pull the prepared bruschetta into chunks or large pieces and place in a bowl.

Halve the tomatoes and squeeze the seeds and juice through a sieve into a separate bowl. Discard the seeds and keep the juice for the dressing. Break up the tomatoes.

Rip half the basil into a mortar, along with the garlic and a good pinch of salt. Pound to a pulp. Add the red wine vinegar and reserved tomato juice. Gradually add the olive oil and adjust the seasoning.

Combine the broken bread with the broken tomatoes, then add the basil dressing and squeeze together to combine all the flavours.

To finish, add the rocket and remaining basil leaves, and toss together. Serve straightaway.

Marinated olives

These olives are a great little addition to a barbecue. They can be served as tasty finger food while the meat, fish and veg are cooking, or as a side dish to accompany the main show. They are also delicious on Bruschetta (page 44).

For the best results use a mixture of olives – black and green, large and small – and try to buy them unpitted. If you have any marinated olives leftover they can be puréed with extra-virgin olive oil and made into a tapenade.

MAKES 500 G

100 g manzanillo olives, washed and seeded

100 g kalamata olives, washed and seeded

100 g ligurian olives or niçoise olives, washed and seeded

100 g queen green olives, washed and seeded

zest and juice of 1 lemon

1 fennel bulb, washed and finely sliced

½ cup chopped celery heart (including leaves and stalk)

small handful roughly chopped mint leaves

1 garlic clove, finely sliced

80 ml olive oil

1 teaspoon toasted cumin seeds

1 teaspoon chopped red chilli

Combine the olives with the remaining ingredients and leave to stand for 1 hour.

The olives will keep for up to 1 week in the refrigerator if stored in an airtight container but are best eaten within a few days.

Spiced red bean salad

I do yoga with a Geordie mate of mine called John, who spent a bit of time travelling through India. He cooked a wonderful dinner for me and my wife, and this recipe was part of the meal. I loved a the pure, simple flavours and how they complemented the heat of the meat dishes.

This salad would go brilliantly with any of the spicy dishes in this book, particularly the Barbecued Pepper Chicken Curry (page 173), Jerked Chicken (page 168–9) and the sweet, smoky flavour of Classic Barbecued Sticky Ribs (page 154–5) and Pamplona Chicken (page 170–1).

SERVES 4

400 g can kidney beans, rinsed and drained

1 red onion, finely sliced

2 teaspoons toasted cumin seeds

1 bunch coriander, leaves and stems washed and chopped

salt

freshly ground black pepper

juice of 1 lemon

Place the kidney beans and sliced onion in a large bowl.

Add the toasted cumin seeds, then toss the chopped coriander through the salad.

Season with salt, pepper and lemon juice.

Coleslaw

Coleslaw is one of those dishes that has had so many variations over time that the true original has been lost – and I'm certainly not saying that this is it!

Needless to say, coleslaw has become part of barbecue folklore, as it goes so well with barbecued meat and fish. Originally, before the invention of mayonnaise, it was made with a vinegar-based dressing. This recipe gives a healthy twist to the mayo-based varieties around these days. If you prefer mayo, then knock yourself out and use it! I prefer to use firm white cabbage but you can substitute savoy or use red cabbage for colour.

SERVES 8

125 ml cider vinegar

½ cup sugar

800 g white, savoy or red cabbage

3 large celery stalks

1 tablespoon Dijon mustard

½ teaspoon celery seeds

2 firm red apples, finely sliced into matchsticks

3–4 tablespoons Greek yoghurt

½ cup roughly chopped mint leaves

salt

freshly ground black pepper

Place the vinegar and sugar in a small saucepan and bring to the boil to dissolve the sugar. Remove from the heat and allow to cool.

While the vinegar mix is cooling, finely slice the cabbage and celery using a sharp knife or a Japanese mandolin.

When the vinegar mixture has cooled, add the mustard and celery seeds, then combine with the cabbage and celery. For the best results, leave this to stand overnight in order to extract the most flavour. Otherwise, allow it to stand for at least 2 or 3 hours.

Before serving, add the apple, yoghurt and mint leaves, and season to taste.

Carrot salad

When I was travelling through Morocco, I loved seeing the donkeys pulling little carts full of carrots, coriander and parsley, hustling their way through the open markets and souks. Carrot salad is very common in Morocco, and the subtlety of its flavour marries well with North African–style brazier-cooked lamb kofte and skewers.

This is a great salad and it is so easy to make. The secret is in the cooking of the carrots; they have to be done whole, as this way they retain more of their sweetness and taste. Also, try to choose carrots that are organic and fresh, with a good snap. Crushing the garlic with salt keeps the flavours subtle.

SERVES 6

1 kg carrots, washed and peeled

salt

3 garlic cloves, peeled

1½ teaspoons toasted cumin seeds

1 teaspoon honey

juice of 1 lemon

2 teaspoons raisins

2 teaspoons pine nuts, lightly toasted

1 bunch coriander, washed and chopped

olive oil

freshly ground black pepper

Boil the carrots in salty water until tender. Drain, and allow to cool a little so you can slice them into similar sized pieces.

Place the garlic cloves in a mortar and crush with a little salt.

Add the toasted cumin seeds and continue to pound just a little to combine the flavours.

Add the honey and lemon juice. Combine, then toss the carrots thoroughly in the garlic mixture. Add the raisins, pine nuts and coriander.

Dress with a little olive oil, season with pepper and allow to stand at room temperature for 1 hour or so to let the flavours settle together.

Serve the salad at room temperature.

Tabouli

You can't have Lebanese food without tabouli. It's the heart and soul of the meal. Serve the fresh flavours of flat-leaf parsley, lemon, burghul wheat and chopped tomato with lovely flat breads, hummus and grilled marinated meats. Talk about healthy and delicious!

SERVES 4

1 cup soaked fine burghul

3 garlic cloves, chopped

1 large bunch flat-leaf parsley, washed and roughly chopped

250 g tomatoes, halved, seeded and chopped

juice of 1 large lemon

salt

freshly ground black pepper

Wash and prepare the burghul as recommended on the packet (generally, place the burghul in a bowl, cover with cold water and set aside for one hour to soak).

Mix the garlic and parsley in a bowl, then add the chopped tomatoes.

Drain and add the burghul and lemon juice, and combine. Season with salt and pepper.

Kimchi

Kimchi is the cornerstone of a Korean barbecue. Traditionally, it's served as a side dish and in dishes such as kimchi jjigae (kimchi soup). Kimchi is fermented pickled vegetables (commonly Chinese cabbage, radish, garlic, red pepper and spring onions), plus chilli, ginger and salt. It has great health properties and is wonderful for the digestion. Other cultures have something similar; for example, sauerkraut from Germany.

If you're going to attempt a Korean barbecue you *have* to have kimchi. You can buy it from Asian grocery stores, but why not try making it yourself? The great thing about this recipe is that the kimchi lasts for ages, and is at its best after six months. It's a long time to wait but it gives you time to plan your Korean barbecue!

MAKES 500 G

1 large Chinese cabbage, chopped into 5 cm slices
100 g good-quality sea salt
8 spring onions, finely chopped
4 garlic cloves, peeled
2 tablespoons hot chilli powder
1 heaped teaspoon grated ginger
1 tablespoon sugar

Wash the chopped cabbage. Drain, then sprinkle with salt and allow it to stand for a minimum of 2 hours.

Rinse the cabbage and squeeze out all the excess liquid. Place the cabbage in a large bowl and add the spring onions, garlic, chilli powder, ginger and sugar. Toss so the cabbage pieces are well coated with the other ingredients, then pack into a large sterilised glass jar.

Rinse the bowl that held the cabbage with hot water and swish it around to pick up all the flavours. Pour into the jar and seal with a tightly fitting lid. Place in a cool room for 2–3 days to start the fermentation process, then refrigerate or leave in a cool dark cupboard for a minimum of 2 months. For best results, leave for 6 months.

Som tam: green papaya salad

I love the flavours of Thai food – the insatiable heat, and the distinctive combination of sweet, salty and sour. It's like a sensory running of the bulls! Those machismo-destroying little birdseye and prik kii nuu (mouse-dropping) chillies can reduce a grown man to tears, but the exhilaration gets your endorphins rising.

I think the use of unripe fruit is so interesting, and often wonder what prompted people to use fruit in this way. The crunchy freshness of the green papaya adds such a great textural dimension to this salad. And believe me, with six chillies in this recipe, you'll need it! Use fewer chillies if you prefer less heat.

Som tam is often served with one of my favourite barbecued chicken dishes, Gai Yang (page 165), along with sticky rice. The salad has quite a liquid consistency, but the juices are lovely soaked up by the rice and chicken.

SERVES 4

2 medium-sized dark green papaya, peeled and grated

1 cup green beans, chopped into 2 cm lengths

6 green birdseye chillies

3 garlic cloves, peeled

25 g dried shrimps, rinsed in hot water and drained

50 g unsalted roasted peanuts

3 tablespoons lime juice

25 ml fish sauce

10 ml tamarind juice

2 ripe tomatoes, quartered

Rinse the grated papaya in cold water and drain. Combine with the chopped green beans.

Combine the chillies and garlic in a mortar, and pound to a paste.

Separately, pound the shrimps with the peanuts. You want a crumbly texture, not a paste.

Combine the lime juice, fish sauce and tamarind juice with the chilli and garlic. Check the seasoning: you may need to add more fish sauce or lime juice, as the salt and sour flavours need to be evenly balanced.

Add the papaya and beans to the dressing, along with the tomatoes. Gently pound to just soften the papaya.

To serve, top with the shrimps and peanuts.

FISH AND SHELLFISH

I was pretty lucky as a kid, growing up in north-west Western Australia in the coastal town of Port Hedland. At first sight you wouldn't think much of the place, with its causeway of salt flats, the huge mountain of salt, stained ochre by the iron-ore dust, and the small but massively industrialised town at the port.

But appearances were inconsequential to me as a kid. The things that were important to me were the playgrounds I enjoyed: the mangrove swamps and creeks, the beaches, the rocky outcrops and the reefs exposed for kilometres at low tide. I would spend afternoons and weekends fishing, spearing and netting, using any means necessary to catch creatures of the sea.

These expeditions would end with us cooking our catch. We would collect flotsam from the dunes, strewn by many cyclones, to build impromptu barbecues with sheets of corrugated iron or rusted car bonnets, or just throw whole fish straight into the fire. The images and sense of freedom these memories conjure up are beautiful, just like the flavours of the fish. The innocence of that time and the simplicity of our cooking technique is really what made the moment, but around the world for millennia this was how it was done. You just can't beat it.

Whole fish Thai style

The inspiration for this dish comes from my wife and from David Thompson. I have known David since I was a young chef working in Sydney, and my wife worked for David as a junior restaurant manager at Nahm in London, and has travelled extensively through Thailand. Between them, they have prompted my obsession with Thai food.

This dish works best with a nice white-fleshed reef fish – a pan-sized snapper, coral trout or even a tasty bream. It's best to use a fish basket and cook over the direct heat of coals or gas.

The best and simplest way to serve the fish would be with plain steamed rice and Green Papaya Salad (page 105) to balance the sweet flavours.

SERVES 4

1 whole fish (up to 2 kg) a snapper is used here, scaled and cleaned (ask your fishmonger to do this)

sunflower oil

5 tablespoons Thai Sweet Chilli Jam (page 27)

2 kaffir lime leaves, very finely sliced, to garnish

2 tablespoons chopped coriander leaves to garnish

1 lime, cut into wedges to garnish

MARINADE

5 coriander roots, washed and chopped

8 garlic cloves, peeled

5 Thai pink shallots, peeled

1 birdseye chilli

1 tablespoon minced turmeric or turmeric powder

2 tablespoons freshly ground white pepper

3–4 tablespoons fish sauce to taste

2–3 tablespoons lime juice to taste

¼ cup coconut cream (skim off the top of a cold can of coconut milk)

Using a sharp knife, cut incisions along both sides of the fish, about 1 cm apart.

To make the marinade, place all the ingredients in a food processor and blend until smooth. Rub the fish with the marinade and place in the refrigerator for 30 minutes while you prepare your barbecue for direct cooking over a medium–high heat.

Lightly oil the fish basket. Place the fish inside then close and secure the basket. Place over direct heat and cook for 8 minutes on one side, then turn the fish basket over and cook for another 8 minutes.

Meanwhile, warm the chilli jam with a little water to make a brushable paste. When the fish has cooked, brush the fish liberally with the chilli jam paste and cook for a further 1–2 minutes on each side.

Remove the fish from the basket. Brush with any remaining jam and serve garnished with kaffir lime leaves, coriander and lime wedges.

Ben's childhood fish

This is not so much a recipe as a memory.

FEEDS 2 HUNGRY 10-YEAR-OLDS

1 whole fish (perhaps a 700 g large bream), gutted, scales left on
seaweed

Build a fire and allow it to burn down to coals.

Stuff the fish with fresh seaweed – don't use old seaweed that's been washed up on the beach for a week!

Make a bed of even-sized, largish coals so the fish is kept out of the ash and dirt. Place the fish on top of the coals and cook for 6–8 minutes.

Using a stick, turn the fish over and cook for another 5–6 minutes.

The hard part is getting the fish off the coals and onto a flat stone. Use the seaweed to cover the stone like a plate. Pick off the blackened skin and get stuck in.

Cape Town kingfish fillets

I spent four months living in Cape Town, and I fell in love with the place. I couldn't believe the physical and spiritual energy of the Atlantic Ocean, poised at the point where it collides with such force into the Indian Ocean; the awesome surf and the insidious presence of every surfer's worst nightmare, the great white shark.

I remember cooking a meal for some Aussie mates in a wonderful cottage overlooking First Beach near Camps Bay. It was the first time I had ever cooked kingfish on the barbecue and it was sensational.

Kingfish is an oily, dark-fleshed fish, a little like tuna. It is highly prized as a sashimi fish and is high in natural fats such as omega 3 and 6. When chargrilled over a high heat and cooked medium, it is even better than tuna in my book. Watch it though, as overcooking has the tendency to dry it out. Try to buy fillets that are a similar size so they'll cook in the same amount of time. They'll go brilliantly with Anchovy and Rosemary Sauce (page 15).

SERVES 6

6 large (250 g) kingfish fillets
freshly ground black pepper
sea salt crystals or fine rock salt

Prepare your barbecue for direct grilling over a high heat. Ensure that the grill is clean and oil free.

Season the fish well with pepper and salt.

Place the fillets skin side down on the barbecue and cook for 5 minutes (for thick fillets). Turn over and cook for 2–3 minutes.

Remove from the grill to serving plates and allow to rest. For medium–rare, the fillets should be flaking on the outer part of the meat and just undercooked or translucent in the centre.

Salt-crusted fish in coals

The hard part about cooking a fish whole is controlling the heat so the skin doesn't burn or stick to the grill. Cooking fish in a salt crust solves these problems, and keeps it deliciously moist. I like to serve this with Grilled Verdure Misté (page 70) and a nice Basil Mayonnaise (page 31).

SERVES 10

2 lemons, roughly chopped into 3cm pieces

5 kg rock salt

2 egg whites, lightly whisked

2 tablespoons fennel seeds

1 × 2 kg whole fish (trout, salmon or barramundi), freshly gutted and gills removed

bunch flat-leaf parsley

To prepare the salt crust, place the chopped lemons in a large bowl and add the salt, egg whites and fennel seeds. Mix well.

On a baking tray large enough to hold the fish, use half the salt mixture to make a bed 2–3 cm thick in the shape of the fish, and place the fish on top. Stuff the parsley into the cavity of the fish to prevent the salt from getting in and making the flesh overly salty.

Preheat your gas barbecue to 180–200°C with the hood down or prepare a hot charcoal fire.

Cover the fish with the remaining salt, similar in thickness to the bottom layer of salt. If need be, use scrunched-up foil to make a retaining wall to hold the salt in place.

Place the fish on the barbecue and bake for 40–50 minutes with the lid down. If using coals, make a thin base of charcoal by moving the majority of the coals to the side of the fire. Place the tray onto this base, then pile the coals around the edge and on top of the fish.

Check that the fish is cooked by inserting a small knife or roasting fork into the thickest part of the fish; touch it to your lips and if it's warm, the fish is done. Remove from the heat and allow to rest for 10 minutes before removing the crust.

Use a serrated knife to saw around the salt base, being careful not to cut into the flesh. Lift the top off; it may come away in 1 piece or break into several pieces. Brush any excess salt off the fish with a wet pastry brush.

To serve, peel back the skin and cut down the centre of the fish, removing the flesh in portions. It should be wonderfully moist.

Miso-blackened fish fillets

This recipe features a classic Japanese miso marinade. Actually, it's more like a cure, as the salt and sugar work together to draw the moisture out of the fish. This helps to improve the texture of flaky fish and imparts a wonderful flavour.

Miso marinade was made famous in the West by the restaurant chain Nobu in its legendary black cod recipe. It also works well with chicken and pork, although you will need to leave it to marinate for longer. I use it with Robatayaki Miso Eggplant (page 73) and you can use it as a base to make dressings for salads and sashimi dishes.

SERVES 6

1 quantity Miso Marinade
(page 23)
4 large fillets of flaky fish
(mullaway, shark or even
snapper)
handful of coriander and oregano
to garnish

Pour enough marinade over the fish fillets to cover them well. Cover and leave to marinate in the refrigerator for 8 hours or overnight, turning the fillets several times.

Remove the fillets from the marinade and allow to come to room temperature. Cut into large chunks or cubes and thread onto long metal skewers or pre-soaked bamboo skewers.

Prepare your barbecue for direct grilling over a medium–high heat.

Place the skewers above the coals, so the sugar in the miso marinade caramelises and blackens slightly. Cook for 6–8 minutes, turning the skewers regularly.

To serve, brush with a little unused marinade, and garnish with coriander and oregano.

Kiwi barbecued trout with figs

Mark Gardner, the Kiwi chef I worked with on *Surfing the Menu*, cooked this recipe in the show. I made a joke about him using feijoas (the national fruit of New Zealand – they are *awful*!), so I have taken his recipe and swapped them for figs, a fruit that other people in the world will eat! One thing though: you'll need to use New Zealand trout because it's the only place that produces them big enough for this recipe. You'll also need to have butcher's string on hand.

As this dish is such a fantastic statement of what Kiwi food is all about – fresh and exciting combinations of flavours – I suggest that you serve the trout with Baked Sweet Potatoes (page 83), washed down with a Southern Cross Pimm's (page 225), to maintain the theme.

SERVES 6

8 kaffir lime leaves

1 whole trout (2 kg) or small salmon, cut into 2 fillets and pin boned

3 limes

4 ripe figs, thickly sliced

1 tablespoon soft brown sugar

1 cup roughly chopped mint leaves

1 cup roughly chopped flat-leaf parsley

¼ cup toasted pine nuts

sea salt

freshly cracked black pepper

extra lime wedges

Cut 4 lengths of butcher's string making sure they are long enough to tie around the fish and line them up, evenly spaced. Position a lime leaf in the centre of each piece of string, then place 1 fillet of trout or salmon on top, skin-side down. Make sure all the bones have been removed, then squeeze the juice of 1 lime over the flesh.

Place slices of fig along the fillet, dust with brown sugar and squeeze on some more lime juice. Sprinkle over the chopped herbs, followed by the pine nuts, and season with salt and pepper.

Place the remaining fillet on top of the seasoned fillet and tie the string firmly. Slip the remaining kaffir lime leaves under the string, and season well with salt and pepper.

Prepare your barbecue for direct grilling over a medium–high heat.

Cook the fillet for 6–8 minutes, then turn and cook for a further 5–6 minutes.

Allow to rest and serve with lime wedges.

Indian spice-crusted fish

This spice crust is fantastic. It's a sidestep away from your usual breadcrumb and nut combination, using dhal (dried white and yellow split peas). On occasion I have used crushed chickpeas, and then it becomes more like a falafel crust. You can use the mixture with chicken breasts, but I think it's the perfect complement to a white fish fillet like bar cod. I just loved the texture and flavours of the dhal. It's best to use home-dried curry leaves rather than bought ones for this dish, mainly for colour.

Serve with Spiced Yoghurt (page 162) and Spiced Red Bean Salad (page 100), or with a nice sweet tomato relish to balance the spiciness of the fish.

SERVES 4

4 thick bar cod fillets
vegetable oil
lime wedges

MARINADE

2 pinches of salt
2 teaspoons chilli powder
juice of 1 lime
1 teaspoon sugar
2 teaspoons garlic paste
2 teaspoons ginger paste

CRUST

180 g white split peas (urad dal)
1 tablespoon yellow split peas (chana dal)
1 teaspoon fennel seeds
½ teaspoon cumin
1 teaspoon black peppercorns
½ teaspoon chilli flakes
20 freshly dried curry leaves
2 tablespoons chopped coriander leaves

Place all the marinade ingredients in a food processor and purée. Rub the fish fillets with the marinade.

Toast the crust ingredients, except the curry leaves and coriander, in a pan until the split peas turn golden and the spices release their aromas. Leave to cool, then pound in a mortar until you have a fine crumb. Crumble in the curry leaves and chopped coriander.

Roll the fish in the crust mixture.

Prepare your barbecue for direct grilling over a medium–high heat.

Add vegetable oil and cook the fish for 4–5 minutes on one side, then turn and cook for 3–4 minutes on the other.

Serve with lime wedges.

Snowy Morrison's hot smoked salmon

 I named my son after my mate Herb (aka Stephen) Barrett, who grew up on the west coast of Tasmania. We spent some time with Herb and his family when we were filming *Surfing the Menu*, and were introduced to a long-time family friend called Snowy Morrison.

Snowy is a legend. He runs the wood mill down in Strahan, and while we were filming with him he made some of the most amazing hot smoked salmon I have ever tasted. We asked Snowy in vain to give up his recipe. Finally, with the help of Herb, I uncovered the long-kept secrets of this old dog's smoked salmon.

For the real deal you'll need to get your hands on some Tasmanian cheesewood woodchips, but Snowy says you can use a fruitwood like cherry or apple. I've had great success with Jack Daniel's wood smoking chips made from the barrel. Whichever woodchips you use, they'll need to be pre-soaked. You'll also need a kettle barbecue, as that's what Snowy uses.

SERVES 4

4 × 200 g thick salmon fillets, bones removed, skin left on

1 tablespoon dark rum

SNOWY'S SECRET RUB

1 tablespoon soft brown sugar

1 tablespoon Cajun Spice (page 36)

1 tablespoon salt flakes

1 tablespoon tomato sauce

1 tablespoon low-salt soy sauce

To make the rub, combine the brown sugar, Cajun spice and salt, then mix in the sauce and soy sauce.

Wash the salmon with the rum and leave to marinate for 30 minutes. Massage in the secret rub and leave to marinate in the refrigerator for 2 hours.

Remove the salmon from the refrigerator and allow it to come to room temperature.

Prepare a kettle barbecue for indirect cooking, building a small coal fire on both sides of the grill and allowing it to burn quite low until almost out. Add 2 handfuls of pre-soaked woodchips to both sides and allow them to start smoking well, with the lid on. If you have a thermometer, the temperature should be around 80–100°C.

Place the salmon on the grill, away from the heat source. Replace the lid and smoke for 40 minutes. Do not lift the lid, because if you're looking, you're not cooking!

Check the fish after 40 minutes, when it should be just cooked. Remove from the barbecue and allow it to rest before serving.

Sicilian sardines in oil

Being a Western Australian, I love our famous sardines. It's no surprise that the Sicilians who migrated to WA felt right at home, and I am sure they kept the sardines their secret for some time.

I picked up this recipe from a fisherman in Fremantle by the name of Jim. It's a classic Italian recipe, using a technique called *sott'olio*, which means 'under oil'. The fish is simply grilled, seasoned and covered in good-quality olive oil.

These sardines are great served with Bruschetta (page 44) and some shaved fennel.

SERVES 6

12 whole sardines, cleaned
salt
freshly ground black pepper
1 tablespoon crumbled wild
  oregano
1 dried chilli, crumbled
1 garlic clove, finely sliced
juice of 1 lemon
250 ml best-quality extra-virgin
  olive oil

Prepare your barbecue for direct grilling.

Season the sardines and place them directly over the fire. Cook on each side for 3 minutes, then transfer to a shallow dish.

Scatter over the oregano, chilli and garlic.

Season with salt, pepper and a squeeze of lemon juice, and cover with olive oil.

Allow to cool and the flavours to mingle before serving.

Paella

Paella is Spain's national dish, and there are as many variations as there are for Italy's risotto. Paella is a celebration of ingredients from the land and the sea, but common to all varieties is saffron, with its beautiful aroma and striking colour.

The reason I have included this recipe here is because the best paellas are cooked in huge pans over the glowing embers of a fire. Excellent results can also be achieved with a good gas or kettle barbecue.

SERVES 4

good pinch of saffron
175 ml white wine
2 tablespoons olive oil
2 chicken thighs, boned and diced
150 g chorizo picante, sliced
1 medium onion, finely diced
100 g celery, finely diced
1 dried chilli, finely chopped
4 garlic cloves, sliced
12 baby octopus, cleaned and washed
250 g paella rice
1 litre chicken stock
150 g broad beans, podded
250 g raw prawns, unpeeled
12 black mussels
12 vine-ripened cherry tomatoes, lightly roasted
salt
freshly ground black pepper
2 tablespoons chopped parsley
2 lemons, halved

Steep the saffron in the white wine for at least 10 minutes.

Heat the olive oil in a large pan or paella dish and sauté the chicken and chorizo until nicely coloured.

Add the onion, celery, dried chilli and garlic, and fry for 2 minutes.

Add the baby octopus, then sprinkle over the rice.

Pour the saffron-infused wine over the rice and allow to evaporate. Add the chicken stock and shake the pan to disperse the ingredients. Add the broad beans, prawns and mussels, and simmer for 15 minutes, shaking the pan every so often but not stirring. If the rice is just tender and the liquid has been absorbed, the paella is ready. If it is a little wet and the rice is still al dente, cook for a further 5 minutes.

Just before you remove the paella from the heat, add the tomatoes and stir them into the rice, turning everything over to plump it up.

To serve, season to taste and garnish with chopped parsley and lemon halves.

Caribbean jerked red fish

 The thing I loved about living in Hackney in London is its cultural diversity. There are Turkish mini-marts, kebab stalls, Chinese restaurants, Vietnamese grocery stores and Nigerian and Ghanaian takeaways. One of the great London foodie landmarks is the Ridley Road Market in Dalston. This recipe is a tribute to the wonderful flavours, sights and sounds of that effervescent market and the fabulous West Indian ingredients available. I especially love the reef fish you can buy there – red fish, rasscasse and red snapper, all with lovely white flesh.

When barbecuing a whole fish it can be difficult to turn it over without pulling off half a fillet, as they tend to stick to the grill. I find it's much easier if you use a fish basket. It's basically a fish-shaped cage that holds your fish and enables you to turn it while the flames and the heat crisp up the skin, and it also allows you to baste your fish while cooking. It's a great thing to take along on fishing and camping trips.

This dish is perfect served with steamed rice and a jug of Rustie Lee's Caribbean Cooler (page 218)!

SERVES 4

1 whole red snapper or similar red reef fish (about 1.5 kg), scaled and gutted

sunflower oil

lime wedges to serve

JERK SPICE

1½ cups chopped spring onions

1 cup chopped coriander leaves

2 Scotch bonnet chillies

3 tablespoons lime juice

1 tablespoon cider vinegar

1 tablespoon brown sugar

2 teaspoons thyme leaves

1 teaspoon ginger paste

1½ taspoons salt

1 teaspoon allspice or ground pimento

1 teaspoon freshly ground black pepper

½ teaspoon nutmeg

½ teaspoon cinnamon

Place all the jerk spice ingredients in a food processor and purée.

Make diagonal cuts into the skin of the fish. Rub in the marinade and leave for 30 minutes.

Prepare your barbecue for direct cooking over a medium–high heat.

Lightly oil the fish basket. Place the fish inside then close and secure the basket. Place over direct heat and cook for 10 minutes on one side, then turn the fish basket over and cook for another 10 minutes.

To test if the fish is cooked, push a skewer through the thickest part of the fish. It should pass through without much force.

Serve with lime wedges.

Grilled lobsters

This recipe was inspired by a New Year's Eve I once spent in Norfolk. In the UK they have fantastic native lobsters with big nippers and wonderfully sweet, tender flesh. We bought four largish lobsters but had little means of cooking them (i.e. pots!). I just added some wet bay leaves, wrapped the lobsters in foil and threw them into the log fire. Awesome.

This recipe has evolved slightly from the original, but it's the simplicity that defines this dish. Its success relies wholly on the availability of top-quality live lobsters. The only thing added is a fresh-flavoured herb and garlic butter. Leftover butter can be wrapped in cling wrap and frozen for future use. It will last for two or three months.

SERVES 2

2 × 800–900 g live lobsters
  or crayfish
salt
freshly ground black pepper
4 bay leaves

HERB BUTTER

250 g unsalted butter, softened
1 tablespoon chopped dill
1 tablespoon chopped chives
1 tablespoon chopped parsley
1 small garlic clove, finely chopped
salt
freshly ground black pepper
2 tablespoons cognac

Kill your lobsters or crayfish by placing them in the freezer for 30 minutes to put them to sleep. Cut in half along the top from head to tail and open into 2 halves. Remove the gravel sack (the blackish tube along the tail).

Season the halves with salt and pepper and push a bay leaf under the flesh of the tail.

To make the herb butter, combine the soft butter with the chopped herbs and garlic, and season with salt and pepper. Beat in the cognac and allow to infuse for 30 minutes.

Prepare your barbecue for direct grilling over a high heat.

Place the lobster halves flesh side down over the heat and cook for 4–5 minutes. Turn them over onto the shell side and continue to cook for 2–3 minutes. The flesh should be nicely charred.

To serve, remove the bay leaves and spoon 1 tablespoon of herb and garlic butter on top of each lobster half. Allow to melt and serve straightaway.

Moreton Bay bugs with figs and pancetta kebabs

I love bugs. They are truly one of the strangest looking crustaceans we eat, but one of the tastiest – in my opinion, second only to wild marron. I cooked this dish on a TV cook-off series called *The Best in Australia*. Personally, I think it should have won! Everything about it works.

This combination of fruit, seafood and meat is quite common in the Mediterranean. Just make sure you have lovely ripe figs and fresh bugs. Ideally, the skewers should be cooked over a charcoal fire but a regular grill will do.

SERVES 4

8 Moreton Bay bugs
200 g thinly sliced dried pancetta
8 bay leaves
4 ripe figs, halved
2 tablespoons olive oil
juice of 1 lemon

Prepare your barbecue for direct grilling over a high heat.

Prepare the bugs by removing the meat from the shells. To do this, remove the head, use a pair of scissors to cut along each side under the tail, then pull out the flesh.

Take 4 metal skewers and thread the following onto each skewer: a bug's tail, some thinly sliced pancetta, a bay leaf and half a fig, then repeat the sequence to complete the skewer.

Brush the skewers with a little oil and place over a high heat to cook until the bugs are translucent, the thin pancetta is crisp and the figs are oozy and caramelised.

To serve, dress with a squeeze of lemon juice.

Scallops with sweet chilli jam

Scallops are one of my favourite shellfish to grill. They have a magical effect at a barbecue – people just can't get enough of them. Here, their sweet, salty flavour is a perfect match with chilli jam, balanced by the freshness of the salad garnish. They are a great little starter or taster to pass around for a sophisticated evening around the flames. Remember to keep the shells for serving.

SERVES 4

12 large king scallops, cleaned and shelled

salt

freshly ground black pepper

sunflower oil

4–5 tablespoons Thai Sweet Chilli Jam (page 27)

1 cup mint leaves

3 kaffir lime leaves, finely sliced

1 stick lemongrass, peeled and finely sliced

1 green chilli (optional), finely sliced

2 limes, halved

Prepare your barbecue hotplate for grilling over a medium–high heat.

Season the scallops just prior to cooking.

Lightly oil the barbecue hotplate and place the scallops on it flat-side down. Cook for 1 minute then turn over.

Spoon on the chilli jam and toss the scallops through it so they are well coated. Remove from the heat after no more than 3 minutes on the grill, less if the scallops are small. High heat is the key to cooking scallops quickly.

Return the jam-coated scallops to their shells. Toss together the mint leaves, lime leaves, lemongrass and green chilli (if using).

To serve, garnish each shell with a little salad and half a lime.

Drunken crabs

When I was a first-year apprentice I worked what we called the backbench, doing the prep for the section chef de parties. Along with a million other tasks, I would spend the services prepping live crabs, soaking them in beer or vodka and setting them up for the chef to cook. You had to stay ahead of the chef, otherwise you would get stuff thrown at you. It wasn't long before I was the section chef doing exactly the same thing, throwing things at the apprentice if he didn't keep ahead! You can cook this dish on a hotplate or in a wok balanced on coals, and it's great served with crusty bread spread with loads of butter.

SERVES 4

4 large blue swimmer crabs or sand crabs, cleaned and halved, claws cracked

375 ml can beer or 100 ml vodka

3 garlic cloves, chopped

2 hot red chillies

2 cups chopped spring onions, white and green parts chopped separately

2 tablespoons olive oil

400 g can chopped Roma tomatoes, drained

1 cup chopped coriander leaves

salt

freshly ground black pepper

Place the cleaned crabs in a bowl with the beer or vodka and leave them to steep for 10 minutes.

Preheat your barbecue hotplate to a high heat. Splash some beer onto the hotplate or wok to check the heat; the beer should evaporate quickly, but let it heat up for a further 5 minutes just to make sure.

Combine the garlic, chillies and white spring onions in a large bowl, together with the marinated crabs.

Pour the olive oil on the hotplate or wok, then add the crabs and pour over the chopped tomatoes. Place a bowl or the lid of the wok over the crabs, then pour the beer or vodka marinade around the edge of the bowl so the liquid seeps underneath and steams them. Allow to steam for 5 minutes. Remove the cover to check how they're going by breaking a section of crab. When the meat is white, toss through the remaining green tops of the spring onions and coriander.

Check the seasoning and remove to a serving plate.

Singapore chilli crabs

I came up with this version of Singapore chilli crab while I was holidaying in Port Douglas, in Far North Queensland. We'd met a couple at the apartments we were staying in, and Glen and I chartered a boat to go fishing. It cost us 120 bucks each for the services of a guide who was more interested in making sure his missus dropped off a change of clothes for him so he could spend the night at the pub that evening!

One mud crab, a reef shark and three hours later, we returned triumphantly with the most expensive shark steaks and mud crab you could imagine. Bearing this in mind, along with the fact that it was Glen's birthday, I thought I'd give the crab the royal treatment. What really helped this recipe was the local sambal I bought at the markets. To replace it you could buy a commercial chilli sauce, but sambal is nice and salty so try to source some from a good Asian food store.

SERVES 4

6 medium to large blue swimmer crabs, cleaned and halved, claws cracked

1 cup chopped spring onions, white part only

250 ml tomato sauce

1 tablespoon sambal

1–2 red Fire-roasted Peppers (page 80), chopped

1 teaspoon chopped ginger

1 teaspoon chopped garlic

100 ml sunflower oil

100 ml beer

salt

freshly ground black pepper

1½ cups finely sliced spring onions, green tops only

1 finely sliced red chilli

Preheat your barbecue hotplate to medium–high.

Place the prepared crabs in a large stainless-steel bowl, along with the white spring onions, sauce, sambal, peppers, ginger and garlic.

Pour the oil onto the hotplate, then add the contents of the bowl. Toss and fry.

Place the bowl over the crabs, then pour beer around the edge of the bowl so it seeps underneath and steams the crabs. Lift up the bowl and toss the crabs to ensure they cook evenly. If necessary, add more beer to continue steaming.

Remove the cover to check how they're going by breaking a section of crab. When the meat is white, they're cooked.

Season with salt and pepper, transfer to a serving dish and garnish with the sliced green spring onion tops and red chilli.

Squid stuffed with fennel and black pudding

Fish and pork are a classic pairing, especially in this Spanish blend of crumbly *morcilla* (blood sausage) and squid. I think it's the spicy flavour and fat content of the sausage that works so well with the squid, and the addition of fennel gives a hint of aniseed to the dish. An alternative to stuffing the squid with the cooked fennel would be to serve the fennel as a shaved salad, with the addition of some mint.

SERVES 4

50 ml olive oil

1 large fennel bulb, finely diced

200 g Spanish blood sausage

salt

freshly ground black pepper

8 medium whole squid, tubes
   cleaned and tentacles trimmed

Prepare your barbecue for direct grilling over a medium–high heat.

Gently fry the fennel in a little olive oil until soft, sweet and slightly golden. Allow to cool.

Remove the blood sausage from its outer skin and crumble onto the cooked fennel. Combine and season with salt and pepper.

Make lots of small cuts along the length of the tubes to about 1 cm deep. This will allow the heat to penetrate the sausage, and it also looks impressive.

Stuff the squid tubes with the sausage and fennel mixture, being careful not to overfill them as the sausage will not heat through thoroughly when cooking. Reserve any leftover sausage mixture.

Once the tubes are stuffed, lightly oil and season the squid tubes. Place them cut-side down on the barbecue and cook for 3 minutes, until nicely charred. Turn over and cook for another 1–2 minutes. If you have any leftover sausage mixture, place it on the barbecue hotplate to cook at this point, along with the trimmed tentacles.

Serve the squid garnished with a sprinkling of any leftover cooked sausage and the cooked tentacles with a light green salad.

MEAT

When our Neolithic forebears used fire

to protect themselves from the wild beasts of the world, I wonder if they had any idea as they were twirling hairy morsels of some prehistoric animal at the end of a stick to consume, in many thousands of years' time people around the world would still be using their techniques to cook slightly more appetising things to eat in their backyards.

For most people, a barbecue is all about meat – duck, chicken, rabbit, cow, pork. I reckon the latter was given to us by God for the sole purpose of barbecuing, it tastes soooo good. Just try Chinese char sui, a Mexican pit *barbacoa* or ribs and pulled pork from the American south, and you'll see what I mean. Then there's Thai chicken and African/Portuguese peri-peri chicken. And how can we forget the wonderful flavours of the perfect grilled steak, the famous bistecca alla fiorentina and the one-day-to-cook Texas beef brisket?

Cooking techniques differ from country to country, and can involve smoking and slow cooking or the fierce direct heat of a coal fire. The asado and churrasco methods of barbecuing meat are perfect examples of direct grilling. These South American styles were created in countries that grew up on the fat of the land and the back of a cow!

Argentinean asado

In the early part of the twentieth century, Argentina produced grain and beef of the highest quality, so it's not too much of a surprise that Argentineans continue to consume a lot of meat.

An asado is a very popular, traditional method of cooking meat, originating in the Pampas regions of Argentina, Uruguay, Chile and Brazil. Typically, a wood fire burning on the ground or in a pit is surrounded by metal cross-stakes upon which the meat is rested, splayed open to receive the heat. The preparation is simple: the meat is merely seasoned with salt before and during the cooking process. It's a slow method of cooking, and the heat and the meat's distance from the fire need to be controlled. The meat juices and fat are never allowed to hit the fire because the smoke will affect the flavour of the meat, and often the fire is cleared from underneath the meat during the proceedings. The meat is generally transferred to a tray and typically served with chimichurri, a herb dressing.

Meat served at an asado is eaten in the following sequence: *morcillas* (blood sausages), chorizos, *chinchulines* (intestines), *mollejas* (sweetbreads) and other organs, followed by the ribs and steaks. Food cooked à la asado is when a parrilla (grill) is placed over coals that have formed from the fire and the meat is then cooked over the slow heat of the coals.

One of my kitchen porters used to reminisce about the asados back home in South America. They would build a big fire on the beach and skewer a whole strip loin on a star picket and then knock it into the ground next to the fire. As the fire burnt down they would move the star picket and the meat closer in until it was cooked. Now *that's* a barbecue!

South American churrasco

Churrasco is a Spanish/Portuguese word that defines the grilling of meat over a wood or coal fire. The definition varies across South America, from Central American countries such as Nicaragua, where it is used to describe long strips of tenderloin beef cooked on skewers and served with chimichurri, to Argentina, where it describes a large cut of beef that forms one of the courses cooked on an asado.

The true identity of the churrasco finds its origins in the southern regions of Brazil, where the Gauchos (cowboys) of the Pampas regions would cook their meat over coals on spikes, as opposed to the grills found in Argentina and Uruguay. This style of cooking found its way via highway eateries and truck stops to the large cities, where the cooking technique became more sophisticated. Typically, the meat is not marinated but simply seasoned with a paste of salt and water brushed onto the meat as it cooks. It really is flame-cooked meat at its purest!

How to cook the perfect steak

Most barbecue lovers are meat junkies, so it stands to reason that most barbecues involve cooking the odd steak. I know there are some criminal meat cooks out there, as I have witnessed some major acts of steak slaughter.

Follow these simple steps and you're guaranteed to end up with the perfect steak every time. It's worth remembering though that the quality of the meat is a huge factor in the tenderness and tastiness of the end product.

The selection of the right cut is important. You're going to need a cut that is tender. The cuts that are best suited to the high heat of direct grilling are of course a well-marinated skirt steak or cuts such as sirloin, porterhouse, T-bone, rump or tenderloin (fillet). All these cuts have a broad surface area that takes advantage of the charred flavour from the high heat.

I recommend that the steaks be allowed to return to room temperature prior to grilling. This not only makes the cooking time shorter but also means that you lose less moisture from your meat.

Season your steaks just prior to grilling with coarsely ground rock salt or quality crystal salt and freshly ground pepper, or with spices if that's what you're using. If added early on, salt will draw moisture from the protein of the meat, which will in turn dissolve the salt. The coarse salt helps to protect the meat from sticking to the grill and also gives a lovely crust to the meat.

Your fire should be built or the gas arranged so you have a hot area and a cooler area so you can move your steak from the high heat to a more steady, lower heat. This is more important if you're cooking large, thick steaks as opposed to thin, quick-cook steaks. Be sure that your grill is clean and free of oil and fat, as they will impart a tainted flavour to your grilled meat. I never oil the steaks or the grill as oil cooking over a high heat will burn and flavour the meat. A hot fire and some seasoning are all you need to stop the steak from sticking.

Now it's time to cook your steaks. The golden rule is to never overcrowd your grill, as too many steaks will absorb the heat and lower the cooking temperature of the grill, especially if you're cooking on gas. Arrange your steaks in a row, in the order in which you plan to cook them. Organisation is the key to grill control.

Allow your steak to seal on the first side for 2–3 minutes, then rotate it 90 degrees so you end up with crisscross grill marks for presentation. You should only turn steaks a maximum of three times (this was something I was taught from a young age as a grill chef). Moisture from the steak will push up through the meat away from the heat. The trick is to create a balance between the two sides of the meat. Heat seals the meat surface, reducing the moisture's chance of escaping. If you allow the steak to remain on one side for too long, all the moisture will push out the other side and you will have a dry steak.

As a general rule, when cooking inch-thick steaks turn them after about 5 minutes and repeat the crisscross cooking on the other side. You will require a little less time on the second side, as the meat will be hotter; allow 3–4 minutes. Give the meat a final turn for just 30 seconds, just to heat the other side once again and to balance the movement of moisture.

To tell how cooked your steak is, the best method is to touch it. You should never cut a steak to check this. I use the finger to thumb method, which replicates the feeling of 'done-ness'. To do this feel the fleshy pad at the base of your thumb which should feel different depending on which finger is gently meeting your thumb. As a rough gauge; thumb and index finger = rare to medium–rare; thumb to middle finger = medium–rare to medium; thumb to ring finger = medium to medium-well-done; thumb to pinkie = medium-well-done to well-done.

The last step is the most important: the resting of the meat. When you cook meat, the protein contracts and the moisture heats up and moves from areas of high heat to lower heat (osmosis). Resting the meat after cooking allows the meat proteins to relax and the moisture that was moving outwards to return and settle within the meat. Rest the meat for half the time you took to cook it.

Aussie steak sandwich

Flank steak is an often-overlooked option when it comes to barbecuing. Cut from the belly, it is substantially tougher than rump or sirloin and benefits from being marinated and tenderised. Ideally, this recipe should marinate for two days. For this reason it has a far better flavour than most grilling steaks.

Flank steak is popular in France, where it is known as *bavette*, and also in Mexico, where it's called *arrachera* and is used in tortillas, and in Texas it is cooked slowly, like you would a brisket. I prefer the good old Aussie way! Marinate it really well and then just show it the fire. Cook it quickly and cut it thin, and you will enjoy the best steak sandwich this side of the black stump.

SERVES 6

1 kg skirt or flank steak, trimmed of sinew but leave the fat

12 pieces of Turkish bread

2 vine-ripened tomatoes, sliced

2 handfuls rocket

MARINADE

2 garlic cloves, minced

2 long red chillies

250 ml olive oil

2 tablespoons sherry vinegar

2 tablespoons Worcestershire sauce

1 tablespoon canned chopped tomatoes

100 ml kecap manis

1 teaspoon freshly ground black pepper

2 tablespoons thyme leaves

ONION CONFIT

75 g butter

5 large onions, finely sliced

1 tablespoon sugar

sprig of rosemary

HONEY–MUSTARD MAYONNAISE

4 tablespoons Mayonnaise (page 30)

1 tablespoon Dijon mustard

½ tablespoon runny honey

Prepare the marinade by combining all the ingredients in a food processor and blitzing. Rub into the trimmed steak and leave to marinate in the refrigerator overnight, but for the best flavour for 2 days.

Prepare the onion confit by melting the butter over a low heat. Add the sliced onions, sugar and rosemary, and cook slowly until soft, golden and sweet. The confit can be made in advance and will keep for 1 month in the refrigerator if stored in an airtight container.

To make the honey–mustard mayo, simply combine all ingredients well.

Remove the meat from the marinade, pat it dry and allow to come to room temperature.

Prepare your barbecue for direct grilling over a high heat. I recommend that you cook the steak to medium–rare and no more (see page 143). Once cooked, allow the steak to rest.

Place the marinade in a small saucepan and reduce.

Toast slices of Turkish bread on the grill on one side only, so you get crunch but not dryness.

To make each steak sandwich, spread the untoasted side of the bread with onion confit, add tomato and rocket, and dress with the mayonnaise. Slice the meat thinly, dress with the reduced marinade, place on top of your salad and top with a slice of toasted bread.

Bistecca alla fiorentina

 This beef cut is an Italian cultural icon, one of the most famous steaks in the world. You cannot travel to Tuscany and not see it on the menu. It's known to most people around the world as another cut altogether, porterhouse steak, and is composed of the loin and tenderloin of beef attached to the bone. It's similar to the T-bone but with a greater portion of fillet attached.

Traditionally, the meat for bistecca alla fiorentina is obtained from a breed of animal known as the chianina (pronounced 'kee-a-nee-na'). These cattle have been bred for twenty-two centuries in the Val di Chiana region, particularly the areas surrounding Siena and Arezzo, making it one of the oldest breeds in existence. The size of this steak provides more than enough meat for two or three people to share. As with most Italian cuisine, the quality of the meat and the simplicity of the preparation make this dish stand out.

SERVES 2–3

1–1.5 kg porterhouse steak

coarse sea salt

2 tablespoons best-quality extra-virgin olive oil

1 garlic clove, smashed

2 sprigs of rosemary, bruised

freshly ground black pepper

Ask your butcher to cut a nice thick steak for you, untrimmed and about 3 fingers thick. Before cooking, allow the steak to come to room temperature so it isn't chilled in the middle. This will allow it to cook more evenly.

Prepare your barbecue for direct grilling, with one area of the grill hotter than the other. Season the steak with salt and place it over the hottest part of the barbecue.

Cook the steak to a good colour on either side for 5–10 minutes, then move to the lower heat to finish cooking. The thickness of the steak and the fact it is still on the bone will mean you will always have parts that are more cooked than others. Towards the bone will be rare and the outer portions will be medium–well-done.

Once you are happy with the degree of cooking, remove the steak to a tray into which you have placed the olive oil, garlic and rosemary. Allow the steak to rest in the tray for 10 minutes, turning it in the infused oil.

Carve the 2 sections of meat from the bone and slice. To serve, arrange the steak on a serving platter with the bone, season with salt and pepper, and drizzle with the oil and meat juices.

Beef brisket Texas-style

There are two schools of barbecuing in the US: east of the Mississippi pork is the rock'n'roll of barbecues, while in Texas it's all about beef. This is a pretty straight up recipe, just stick the meat in a bun with some delicious Coleslaw (page 101) and Basic Barbecue Sauce (page 14). You'll need to have half a dozen cups of woodchips on hand for this recipe.

SERVES 10

3 kg untrimmed brisket, the fattier
  the better
250 ml beer or water

RUB
1 tablespoon rock salt
3 tablespoons soft brown sugar
1 teaspoon crushed dried chillies
½ teaspoon five-spice powder

Combine the rub ingredients in a bowl.

Trim the brisket of any dry and unclean parts of meat. Cut the fat with a sharp knife in a crisscross fashion to allow the fat to render down and also so the rub can penetrate.

Rub the brisket with the sugar mix and leave to marinate in the refrigerator overnight.

Remove the brisket from the refrigerator and allow it to come to room temperature.

Now, the big job is getting the fire right. Whether you're using coals or gas, make sure you have enough fuel! Prepare your barbecue for indirect cooking over a medium–low heat, adding a handful of coals every hour to maintain the heat. Place the brisket in a roasting tray, fat-side up, in the centre of the barbecue, away from any direct heat. If the fire is initially too hot, pour on a little beer or water into the tray to prevent any burning and also to help maintain the moisture in the brisket. Add ½ cup of pre-soaked hickory or mesquite chips to each side of the coals and pull down the hood on the barbecue. Now you just need to maintain the heat and add some woodchips each time you replenish the coals.

If using a gas barbecue, light the outer gas burners. Heat some pre-soaked woodchips in a smoke box prior to adding the brisket with the gas on high; when the woodchips start to smoke, turn the heat down, place the brisket on the grill racks between the gas burners and cook on a medium–low heat.

Cook the brisket for about 5 hours, basting with the tray juices until the meat is nice and tender and flakes under a fork. Once cooked, you can pull the meat or thinly slice it.

Pour the tray juices over the meat and serve.

Malay satay beef

Satay recipes have drifted from the Asian subcontinent to the Far East and onwards. This is such an easy and satisfying dish to prepare, and kids and adults alike love it.

The use of papaya in this recipe is interesting as it contains an enzyme that helps to tenderise meat, allowing you to use tougher, tastier cuts like skirt steak.

Serving a satay is the perfect way to get a party started. Prepare a load of satay skewers and serve them to your guests while the main dishes are cooking. They can be cooked quickly over high heat; just make sure you pre-soak your skewers and have a lot of satay sauce on hand.

SERVES 6

500 g skirt steak, cut into strips
1 quantity Satay Sauce (page 28) to serve

MARINADE

20 g papaya
juice of 1 lemon
2–3 garlic cloves, peeled
5 tablespoons yoghurt
75 g chopped chillies
1 tablespoon ground turmeric
salt to taste

Place the marinade ingredients in a food processor and blitz until smooth.

Pour the marinade over the strips of beef and leave in the refrigerator overnight, or for at least 2 hours.

Remove the steak from the refrigerator and allow it to come to room temperature.

Prepare your barbecue for direct grilling over a high heat. Thread the marinated strips of beef onto pre-soaked skewers and cook for 4–5 minutes.

Serve with satay sauce on the side.

Bulgogi: Korean barbecued beef

Bulgogi is one of Korea's most popular barbecued beef dishes. The word means 'fire meat', and it's often served as an introduction to Korean food for those who are unfamiliar with this style of cooking.

Bulgogi is served with various condiments and wrapped in salad leaves, quite similar to the Chinese san choy bow. As in many Asian cuisines, there is a sense of balance and harmony in a bulgogi, with the flavours of the healthy kimchi, spicy ssamjang and fresh lettuce and herbs.

SERVES 6

500 g rump or sirloin steak, sliced

3 tablespoons brown sugar or palm sugar

125 ml light soy sauce

4 garlic cloves, finely chopped

good pinch of salt

100 ml rice wine or mirin

2 tablespoons sesame oil

1 tablespoon toasted sesame seeds

1 bunch spring onions, finely sliced

sunflower oil

1 medium carrot, washed, peeled and finely sliced

½ iceberg lettuce, washed and separated into leaves

1 butterleaf lettuce or lollo rosso lettuce

3 tablespoons Ssamjang (page 23)

200 g Kimchi (page 104)

1 cup picked mint leaves

To make the bulgogi, combine the beef with the sugar, soy sauce, garlic, salt, rice wine or mirin, sesame oil, sesame seeds and spring onions and mix thoroughly. Leave to marinate in the refrigerator for a minimum of 2 hours.

Remove the bulgogi from the refrigerator and allow it to come to room temperature.

Heat your barbecue hotplate to medium–hot. Add a little sunflower oil to the hotplate and quickly fry the marinated meat. Add the carrots and cook to desired tenderness. I like to cook to medium at this stage.

Transfer the bulgogi to a serving dish.

To serve, take a lettuce leaf and add a little ssamjang, kimchi and bulgogi, top with mint leaves and roll up to make a wrap.

Barbecued rib of beef

I've always enjoyed cooking large pieces of meat over coals – I suppose it's the closest I get to cooking Gaucho-style. The cowboys of the Pampas regions of South America are the masters of this style of cooking, impaling large joints of meat and roasting them on an open fire.

This recipe is best followed using an indirect heating method: prepare your coals on one side of your barbecue, or if you have a gas grill pull down the hood, turn your middle gas burners off and crank up the outer gas burners. Add some pre-soaked woodchips for extra flavour.

You'll need to make a brush from lightly bruised sprigs of thyme and rosemary tied together, and use it to brush the ribs with the British beef wash.

SERVES 6

3 kg rib roast (6–8 bones. Ask your butcher to cut off the chin and backbone, leaving just the rib bones)

4 tablespoons Basic Barbecue Sauce (page 14)

BRITISH BEEF WASH

1 tablespoon hot water

1 tablespoon salt

2 tablespoons sherry vinegar

1 tablespoon English mustard

2 tablespoons Worcestershire sauce

If using coals, prepare your barbecue for indirect cooking well in advance so you build up a good heat base. Whether you're using coals or gas, pour a little water into the drip tray underneath the grill to help maintain moisture within the barbecue; you'll need to top it up from time to time.

While the barbecue is heating up, take the rib of beef out of the refrigerator and allow it to come to room temperature. This will help ensure it cooks evenly.

To make the British beef wash, place all the ingredients in a jar and shake to combine. Brush the rib roast with the wash, and give it another good brushing before you start cooking.

Place the beef on the barbecue while it is at its hottest and cover with the hood or lid of the barbecue. After the initial burst of heat (about 15–20 minutes), allow the coals to ease in intensity and maintain this heat by adding a few coals from time-to-time, along with some pre-soaked woodchips for smoke. If using a gas barbecue, turn the gas down slightly to maintain a medium heat. Add a handful of pre-soaked woodchips to the smoke box from time to time to maintain a gentle smoke.

Brush the rib roast liberally with the beef wash at intervals.

A joint of this size will take 1½–2 hours to cook. Allow the fire to burn down during the last 30 minutes of cooking time. At this stage, prepare the barbecue sauce to glaze the beef.

Allow the beef to rest for 20 minutes, then carve, glazing with the sauce.

Classic barbecued sticky ribs

Barbecued ribs conjure up images of classic American barbecues. They're slow-cooked, to achieve meat that's tender, moist and smoky, and finished with a sticky-sweet, sometimes sharp sauce or glaze.

There are thousands of recipes for these babies – there are even world barbecue championships to find the best rib recipes! Some people boil their ribs first but true practitioners of the fine art of barbecuing believe this is a cardinal sin. The only way to achieve perfection is firstly to rub the ribs and then to barbecue them. The rub is generally a mix of salt, sugar and spices, which cures the meat, drawing out excess moisture and concentrating the flavour. The sugar helps to tenderise the flesh and slowly caramelises during the barbecue process to add to the wonderful flavour of the meat.

SERVES 4–6

3–4 kg pork baby back ribs

250 ml apple juice

RUB

1 teaspoon Celery Salt (page 35)

1 tablespoon soft brown sugar

1 tablespoon salt

1 teaspoon chilli powder

1 teaspoon smoked paprika

1 teaspoon freshly cracked black
  pepper

1 teaspoon English mustard
  powder

1 tablespoon onion flakes

1 tablespoon garlic flakes

GLAZE

1 cup brown sugar

250 ml malt vinegar

½ stick cinnamon

1 small dried red chilli, crumbled

250 ml tomato sauce

1 tablespoon Dijon mustard

100 g creamed horseradish

100 ml dark rum

Make the rub by placing the ingredients in a food processor and mixing until fine. Rub over the pork ribs and leave to marinate in the refrigerator for 2–3 hours or overnight. The rub will keep for 1 month if stored in an airtight container but you should use it all in this recipe.

Remove the ribs from the refrigerator and allow them to come to room temperature.

Prepare your barbecue for indirect cooking over low–medium heat (roughly 100–120°C). Add a handful of pre-soaked woodchips to the coals, place the ribs over a drip tray and cook with the lid on until soft and tender, or until the bone pulls away from the meat. This will take 2–3 hours to do properly. Add woodchips every 40 minutes or so to keep the gentle smoke flavour going. You will need about 6–8 handfuls of soaked woodchips for this one.

If using a gas barbecue, light the outer gas burners. Heat some pre-soaked woodchips in a smoke box prior to adding the ribs with the gas on high; when the woodchips start to smoke, turn the heat down, place the ribs on the grill racks between the gas burners and cook on a low–medium heat as above.

Spray the ribs with apple juice from time to time to keep them moist.

While the ribs are cooking, combine the glaze ingredients in a saucepan and bring to the boil. Simmer until thick then keep warm.

Once the ribs are cooked, cut them between the bones and place in a dish. Toss through the glaze then return the ribs to the barbecue, this time over direct heat to get them nice and hot and sticky.

Transfer to a serving dish and eat straightaway.

Thai beef salad

When my wife Dee and I are watching what we eat, or we feel like eating something that makes us feel good about ourselves, this one's a no-brainer. It's the perfect detox treatment. I love the clean, fresh flavours, and the heat to get the heart pumping, plus it's so quick to put together.

The Thais did not invent the barbecue but they've come up with some of the best barbecue recipes in the world. I nearly always save a couple of steaks for this salad so I can serve something a bit different when I put on a barbecue. It's ideal served with steamed rice to help cool things down.

SERVES 4

2 bunches spring onions, washed, outer leaves removed, roots and tops trimmed

3 red chillies, finely sliced

10 Thai pink shallots, finely sliced

1 bunch coriander, washed and chopped

3 sticks lemongrass, peeled and thinly sliced

400 g rump or sirloin steak

salt

freshly ground black pepper

juice of 3 limes

5 tablespoons fish sauce

Finely slice the spring onions on the diagonal and place in a bowl with the chillies, shallots, coriander and lemongrass.

Prepare your barbecue for direct grilling over a high heat. Season the beef with a good amount of salt and pepper, then cook to your liking. I prefer medium–well-done as I think you get a more flavourful salad. Allow the meat to rest while you dress the salad.

Squeeze the lime juice over the spring onion salad, followed by the fish sauce, then toss to combine. Slice the meat finely, removing the fat. Add to the salad, toss to combine the flavours and serve.

Bun bo: Vietnamese grilled beef and noodle salad with lemongrass

I have included this recipe because it's one of my wife's favourites. Travelling through Vietnam she fell in love with the food and its fresh flavours. I love this dish because it's quick and simple, and tastes just awesome. Skirt, flank or even sirloin steak is marinated, grilled and finely sliced, then served with this wonderfully refreshing salad. It's close to a Thai beef salad but you don't need to cook any rice.

SERVES 6

500–600 g skirt or flank steak
250 g vermicelli rice noodles

MARINADE

5 shallots, peeled and finely sliced
3 garlic cloves, peeled
2 fat sticks lemongrass, peeled and finely chopped
pinch of salt
1 teaspoon freshly ground white pepper
½ teaspoon turmeric powder
fish sauce to taste

GARNISH

1 medium cucumber, peeled, seeded and finely sliced
200 g bean shoots
½ bunch coriander leaves, chopped
½ bunch mint leaves, chopped
100 g roasted unsalted peanuts
½ iceberg lettuce, chopped
1 quantity Nuoc Cham Sauce (page 29)
chopped red chillies

Make the marinade by pounding the shallots, garlic, lemongrass and pinch of salt in a mortar or food processor until puréed. Add the pepper, turmeric and fish sauce. Rub the marinade into the steak and leave to marinate in the refrigerator overnight if possible, or for at least 2 hours.

Prepare the vermicelli noodles by adding them to a saucepan of boiling water and cooking for 2–3 minutes. Drain, refresh with cold water and drain again.

Divide the noodles between bowls or on a platter.

Remove the steak from the refrigerator and allow it to come to room temperature.

Prepare your barbecue for direct grilling over a high heat. Cook the beef to medium at the most. Rest, then slice thinly.

Place the beef with its juices on top of the noodles, along with the garnishes. Dress well with nuoc cham sauce, then toss together.

Serve with freshly chopped chillies and extra nuoc cham sauce on the side if desired.

Lamb kofte

 Throughout North Africa and the Middle East, kofte generally refers to lamb mince, either in meatball form or squashed by hand onto long skewers and cooked over braziers. I have encountered other meat varieties such as camel and beef but more often than not it is lamb.

Some of my fondest memories of travelling through Morocco are of the souk stallholders busily cooking over charcoal braziers, the smell and the hectic atmosphere as disorienting as they were inspiring. The Djemma el Fnar, a massive square in Marrakech, is just about the best street food market in the world.

I got this recipe from a butcher in Casablanca, merely by observation, and you can use it however you wish. I like to make big lamb burgers using kofte, so I've included the recipe here. I would serve the kofte in wraps instead of buns though.

MAKES 10 KOFTE OR 5 BURGERS

500 g lean lamb, finely minced

2 tablespoons chopped sweet marjoram or oregano

4 tablespoons chopped parsley

4 chopped spring onions

1 teaspoon ground cumin

salt

freshly ground black pepper

1 egg, beaten

Combine the minced lamb with the chopped herbs, spring onions, cumin, salt and pepper, and mix really well.

Add the beaten egg and combine with a wooden spoon until the egg is completely incorporated. Leave to rest for 30 minutes.

Using this mince base you can form small balls that you can squeeze onto metal skewers and cook over hot coals without a grill rack or form into patties to make the Lamb Burgers (opposite).

Lamb burgers

SERVES 5

1 quantity Lamb Kofte (opposite),
  formed into 5 patties
½ bunch mint, leaves chopped
5 tablespoons natural yoghurt
salt
freshly ground black pepper
1 cos lettuce, chopped
1 bunch coriander, leaves picked
juice of 1 lemon
5 wraps
3 tomatoes, sliced
5 tablespoons Harissa (page 22)

Prepare your barbecue for direct grilling over a medium–high heat.

Place the patties on the barbecue and cook on one side, without moving, for 6–8 minutes. Make sure they set and don't crumble; if you try to move them too soon they will fall apart. Turn the patties over and cook for a further 5–8 minutes. You want them to be well cooked; as with any minced or processed product, the chances of food poisoning are greater than with whole cuts of meat.

Mix the chopped mint through the yoghurt and season with salt and pepper.

Toss the cos lettuce with the coriander, dress with lemon juice and season with salt and pepper.

Toast the outsides of the wraps. Arrange the salad and tomato in the centre of the wrap topped with a kofte burger, then add a spoonful of yoghurt and mint, and lashings of spicy harissa.

Lamb shish with chermoula

Shish are generally skewers threaded with chunks of lamb or chicken, cooked over coals. I have seen Greek and Turkish barbecues where they have huge skewers that are turned over coals by an electric rotisserie, but not too many people would have one of them at home! Long metal skewers are easy enough to find, and all you need to do is lift the meat away from the grill bars to get a flame-roasted effect. You can do this by placing two bricks at either end of the grill so you can suspend the skewers over the heat. If you have a kettle barbecue you could balance the skewers on the edge of the barbecue, if your skewers are long enough; if not, just use bricks. Charcoal is by far the best method for this recipe.

SERVES 6

500 g diced leg of lamb

flat bread

6 tablespoons good-quality
   hummus

1 quantity Tabouli (page 103)

olive oil

CHERMOULA MARINADE

3 tablespoons Harissa (page 22)

½ cup chopped parsley

½ cup chopped mint leaves

½ cup chopped coriander leaves

2 garlic cloves, peeled

½ teaspoon ground cinnamon

½ teaspoon ground cumin

1 small lemon, roughly chopped
   and seeds removed

½ cup yoghurt

1 teaspoon sea salt

SPICED YOGHURT

1 cup yoghurt

salt

freshly ground black pepper

½ teaspoon ground cumin

Combine the ingredients to make the chermoula marinade. Place the lamb in the marinade and leave to marinate in the refrigerator overnight.

Remove the lamb from the refrigerator and allow it to come to room temperature. When ready to cook, thread the meat onto metal skewers and refrigerate while you prepare the charcoal for direct grilling over a high heat. If using a gas barbecue, crank it up to the highest setting.

Cook the skewers for as long as you desire. I prefer them to be cooked medium.

While the lamb shish is cooking, make the spiced yoghurt by combining the yoghurt with salt, pepper and cumin.

Warm the flat bread on the grill, then spread with hummus and a large spoonful of tabouli. Place the spiced lamb on top and dress with the seasoned yoghurt and olive oil.

Serve the bread open like a plate or roll it up like a souvlaki.

Grilled rabbit Trapani-style

When I visited Sicily once, I ate an amazing meal at a small trattoria in the port city of Trapani, on the western tip of the island. I can't remember the name of the place, but the two things I do remember were the fantastic antipasti trolley and the huge grill in the kitchen, on which all sorts of wonderful fish and meats were being cooked. Several of our party had baby rabbit, which I must admit was probably the most mouth-wateringly tasty rabbit I have ever eaten. I know it's not very PC to eat baby anything, unless it's octopus, but it was awesome.

On my return to London I ordered the smallest rabbits I could find and put the dish on the menu at the River Café. I love to serve this dish with Refried Beans (page 93).

When buying your rabbits, ask your butcher to split each one down the length of its spine into two halves. Don't trim any belly fat, as this will become lovely and crisp on the barbecue.

SERVES 6

3 small rabbits or 2 larger rabbits (each under 1 kg), split down the spine into 2 halves

2 tablespoons dried wild oregano

1 teaspoon chilli flakes

salt

freshly ground black pepper

2 lemons

½ cup fresh oregano leaves

1 teaspoon salt

160 ml extra-virgin olive oil

Prepare your barbecue for direct grilling over a medium heat.

Dry-rub your rabbits with the dried oregano, followed by the chilli and then with salt and pepper.

Place the rabbits onto the grill, bone-side first. Cook for 10 minutes then turn them over to the skin side and cook for a further 8 minutes until nicely charred and coloured.

Once cooked, remove to a chopping board and using a big chopping knife cut each side into 3 parts: leg, rib section and shoulder. Place on a serving dish with 1 lemon cut into wedges.

In a mortar, pound the fresh oregano with a teaspoon of salt to form a fine green paste. Add the juice of 1 lemon and mix, then add olive oil to make a dressing.

Serve the oregano dressing with the rabbit.

Gai yang: Thai barbecued chicken

My wife spent some time travelling through northern Thailand and Laos, and she still raves about the street food she ate. I asked her if there were any barbecue recipes that stood out from her travels, and without any hesitation she nominated Thai barbecued chicken.

We both love Thai food, so this recipe often makes an appearance at home, served with steamed sticky rice and Som Tam (green papaya salad; page 105), plus Sweet Chilli Sauce (page 26) for extra spice!

SERVES 4

1 × 1.5 kg chicken, cut into 8 joints, trimmed of fat and excess skin

¼ cup coconut cream (skim off the top of a cold can of coconut milk)

MARINADE

5 coriander roots, washed and chopped

6 garlic cloves, peeled

5 Thai pink shallots, peeled

1 birdseye chilli

1 tablespoon minced turmeric or turmeric powder

2 tablespoons freshly ground white pepper

3–4 tablespoons fish sauce to taste

2–3 tablespoons palm sugar to taste

For the marinade, use a heavy mortar and pestle or food processor, and purée the coriander roots, garlic, shallots, chilli and turmeric. Add the pepper, fish sauce and sugar to taste, and mix well.

Rub the marinade into and under the skin of the chicken and leave to marinate in the refrigerator for 2–3 hours.

Remove the chicken from the refrigerator and allow it to come to room temperature.

Prepare your barbecue for direct grilling over a medium heat. Just prior to grilling the chicken, add some pre-soaked woodchips. Once they start to smoke, add the chicken. If using gas, heat the woodchips in a smoke box prior to adding the chicken with the gas on high; when the woodchips start to smoke, turn the heat down and start to cook the chicken.

Cook the chicken for 20 minutes or until cooked through. Combine the leftover marinade with the coconut cream and use this to baste the chicken while you cook, turning the pieces frequently to prevent the sugar burning.

Tandoori chicken

 Tandoori chicken has got to be one of the most instantly recognisable Indian dishes. The famously smoky marinated chicken is traditionally cooked in a terracotta tandoor oven over a charcoal fire.

The history of tandoor ovens reaches back over several thousands of years to Punjab in Pakistan. They are amazing ovens and can reach extreme temperatures. The high heat seals in the flavour and moisture, and imparts a lovely smokiness. Often the meat has a red appearance with touches of black, caused by the intense heat. The red is generally due to the use of red chillies in the marinade, although nowadays annatto, a red food colour, is added.

Tandoori chicken is traditionally served with sliced onion and lemon wedges, and it also goes well with Spiced Red Bean Salad (page 100).

SERVES 4

2 × 1.5 kg chicken, skinned and washed

juice of 1 lemon

1 cm piece of ginger, minced

2 garlic cloves, minced

salt

RED MARINADE

500 g thick yoghurt

5 garlic cloves, minced

3 cm piece of ginger, minced

2 tablespoons sunflower oil

3 teaspoons garam masala powder

2 tablespoons lime juice

100 g red chilli paste

1 teaspoon salt

Make deep cuts into the breast and thigh of the chicken, keeping the bird whole. Alternatively, you could cut through the backbone and flatten the bird with your hands.

Rub the chicken with the lemon juice, ginger and garlic pastes and salt. Cover and leave to marinate in the refrigerator for 1 hour.

Combine the red marinade ingredients in a bowl. Coat the chicken with the marinade, cover and refrigerate for a further 2 hours.

Remove the chicken from the refrigerator and allow it to come to room temperature.

Prepare your barbecue for indirect cooking over a high heat. Place the chicken away from the coals with a tray underneath the meat. Add ½ cup of pre-soaked woodchips to the coals and when they start to smoke, place the lid on the barbecue.

If using a gas barbecue, light the outer gas burners. Heat some pre-soaked woodchips in a smoke box prior to adding the chicken with the gas on high; when the woodchips start to smoke, turn the heat down, place the chicken on the grill racks between the gas burners and cook on a high heat.

Cook the chicken for 45–50 minutes. Maintain the heat at medium–high after the initial hot start, with the addition of a few extra coals to either side if you're using charcoal.

To serve, simply joint the chicken into 4 pieces.

Jerked chicken

The word 'barbecue' originates in the Caribbean. The Taino people of the Caribbean dug pits to cook their food, building fires overlaid with green branches of the pimento tree. The branches formed a rack on which the meat was then cooked.

Things have since moved on somewhat in the Caribbean, and these days it's more common to see barbecues made from old oil barrels cut in half (the same barrels from which they make kettle drums), over which their famous jerk meat is cooked. The thing that makes jerk so great is the use of the aromatic and super-hot Scotch bonnet chilli. Warning! Approach these chillies with caution.

Jerked chicken is great served with Caribbean Rice and Peas (page 91).

SERVES 6

12 chicken thighs
chopped spring onions to garnish

MARINADE

½ bunch spring onions, chopped

¼ bunch coriander, chopped

3 Scotch bonnet or other hot chillies

3 tablespoons tomato sauce

2 tablespoons lime juice

1 tablespoon cider vinegar

1 tablespoon brown sugar

2 teaspoons thyme leaves

1 cm piece of ginger, minced

1½ teaspoons salt

1 teaspoon ground allspice or ground pimento

1 teaspoon freshly cracked black pepper

½ teaspoon ground nutmeg

½ teaspoon ground cinnamon

Trim the chicken thighs of any excess fat and skin. Wash and pat dry.

Combine the marinade ingredients in a food processor and blend until smooth.

Rub the marinade all over the chicken (you might like to wear disposable gloves to do this). Place the chicken in a plastic or ceramic dish to marinate in the refrigerator for at least 3 hours, or overnight if possible.

Remove the chicken from the refrigerator and allow it to come to room temperature.

Prepare your barbecue for direct grilling. Have one side at a medium–high heat and around one-third of the heat source at a lower heat to allow the chicken to cook slowly, preventing the marinade from burning.

Initially, place the thighs over the higher heat to seal and colour the chicken. Add ½ cup of pre-soaked woodchips to the lower heat source, then move the chicken to slowly cook over the lower heat for 15–20 minutes. If using gas, heat your woodchips in a smoke box prior to moving the chicken to cook over the lower heat.

Sprinkle with spring onions and serve while hot.

Pamplona chicken

 Uruguayans cook this fire-roasted dish with pork or chicken, as the cheese and roasted peppers work really well with both types of meat.

The combination of flavours here hints at various European influences. The smoked ham and cheese have a Germanic leaning, while provolone is an Italian speciality cheese and the peppers are a staple at most Italian barbecues.

This chicken is best cooked on charcoal, and it's great served with Chimichurri (page 20) and Fennel Salad (page 85).

SERVES 4

**1 × 1.5 kg chicken, boned flat
(ask your butcher to do this)**

salt

freshly ground black pepper

1 tablespoon dried wild oregano

3 Fire-roasted Peppers (page 80)

**5 slices provolone or mozzarella,
½ cm thick**

100 g smoked ham, thinly sliced

olive oil

Spread out the boned chicken, skin-side down. Remove the breast fillets and arrange them on the breast skin. Season with salt, pepper and wild oregano.

Arrange the fire-roasted peppers over the meat, followed by the cheese and smoked ham.

Roll up the chicken to form a fat Swiss roll and secure with 2 or 3 pre-soaked wooden skewers. Rub the skin with olive oil and season with salt and pepper.

Set up your barbecue for direct grilling over a medium heat.

Place the chicken on the barbecue and cook for 20 minutes, turning frequently to prevent burning. Ensure that the heat is maintained at medium.

When cooked, allow to rest for 10 minutes before carving.

Peri-peri chicken

Cooked with a touch of smokiness, I think this recipe is one of the best barbecue chicken dishes in the world. It has Portuguese roots and is common throughout Africa due to Portugal's colonial interests. Peri-peri is the name used for the African birdseye chilli, and in marinades it usually refers to a beautiful blend of paprika and other spices, combined with the acidity of lime or vinegar. It doesn't have to be outrageously hot.

The peri-peri marinade will keep for up to a week if stored in an airtight container.

SERVES 6

12 chicken thighs, trimmed of excess fat

2 tablespoons olive oil

3 limes, cut into wedges

1 quantity Aioli (page 31)

PERI-PERI MARINADE

2–3 Scotch bonnet or hot chillies, roughly chopped

4 long red chillies, roughly chopped

2 teaspoons sea salt

2 garlic cloves, minced

5 cm piece of ginger, peeled and roughly chopped

2 teaspoons ground coriander

½ teaspoon ground cinnamon

1 teaspoon ground paprika

100 ml white wine vinegar

2 teaspoons chopped oregano

TO SMOKE

1 branch bay

1 large bunch rosemary

1 large bunch parsley

1 bunch thyme

1 bunch sage

To make the marinade, place the chopped chillies and salt in a mortar or food processor and make a paste.

Add the garlic, ginger and spices, and pound or grind to a paste. Add the vinegar and oregano.

Make 2 or 3 slashes in each chicken thigh, cutting to the bone.

Add the chicken to the marinade, cover and leave to marinate in the refrigerator overnight, or for a minimum of 3 hours.

Remove the chicken from the refrigerator and allow it to come to room temperature.

Prepare your barbecue for direct grilling over a medium heat. Barbecue the chicken pieces for 5–8 minutes, just to colour on each side, then remove from the heat. Wet your smoking herbs liberally and place them on the barbecue, arranging the chicken thighs over the top. Continue to cook the chicken with the lid on until cooked through. This may take 20 minutes.

When cooked, drizzle the chicken thighs with olive oil and serve with lime wedges and a spoonful of aioli.

Barbecued pepper chicken curry

This dish started out as a simple curry, but during England's summer festival season I was asked to put on a barbecue over fifteen nights at an open-air festival in Wimbledon. I needed to cook something with a big impact, something that would send out irresistible aromas, so I took this recipe and converted it for the barbecue. Man, it went down a treat!

The only thing you need is a flat griddle plate or you could use a large cast-iron pan on an open fire. It's absolutely fabulous with a cool yoghurt and cucumber dressing, Spiced Red Bean Salad (page 100) or even with the Whole Pumpkin Biryani (page 86).

SERVES 6

6 green chillies (4 long fat ones and 2 short hot ones)

8 garlic cloves, peeled

sunflower oil

juice of 2 large lemons

2 teaspoons ground turmeric

1 × 1.6 kg chicken, jointed for sautéing, skin removed

1 teaspoon cumin seeds

2 medium onions, chopped

2 teaspoons crushed coriander seeds

2 teaspoons freshly cracked black pepper

12 fresh curry leaves

1 cup coriander leaves, chopped

½ cucumber, chopped

5 tablespoons natural yoghurt

salt

freshly ground black pepper

Purée the chillies and garlic in a food processor, adding a little oil if necessary.

Place the chillies and garlic in a bowl with the lemon juice and turmeric. Add the jointed chicken and mix well. Leave to marinate in the refrigerator for a minimum of 2 hours.

Remove the chicken from the refrigerator and allow it to come to room temperature.

Preheat your barbecue hotplate to medium or place a flat griddle pan over the barbecue coals. Pour a little oil onto the barbecue hotplate and start to cook the chicken, turning it so the meat is evenly coloured. Allow the barbecue to burn down to a medium–low heat.

Pour a little more oil onto the hotplate and add the cumin seeds, onions, crushed coriander seeds and black pepper. Fry until the onions start to colour and the aromas of the spices begin to develop. Add the remaining marinade and curry leaves. Continue to cook, turning the chicken until cooked through; this could take 25 minutes in all.

When the chicken is cooked add the coriander.

Combine the cucumber with the yoghurt and season with salt and pepper to taste. To serve, either drizzle the yoghurt over the chicken or serve it separately.

Bender's beer-can chicken

 I don't know who thought up this wicked way of cooking a chicken, but I'm sure it started off as a joke. I have seen it done in both Australia and New Zealand. Obviously, the Kiwis will say that they did it first, and the thing is they probably did. I like to use Japanese Sapporo beer for this recipe.

In his book *The Barbecue Bible*, Grill Master Steve Raichlen writes that he got the inspiration for this technique while attending a world barbecue championship. I suppose everyone has their own method, but one thing I should point out is that you need to open the can of beer or you may find there's not much of your chicken left after the can explodes!

SERVES 6

1 × 1.8 kg chicken

2 tablespoons Chimichurri (page 20)

375 ml can wheat beer

1 lemon, cut into quarters

2 sprigs rosemary

Trim the chicken of any excess fat from the neck end of the bird and the cavity. Remove any giblets. Fold the wing tips in so that they don't hang out.

Rub the chimichurri inside the chicken cavity and between the skin and the meat. Leave the bird to rest while you fire up the barbecue.

Set up your barbecue for indirect cooking, placing a foil tray under the grill.

Open the can of beer and drink a mouthful – just 1 big sip. Push lemon quarters into the can of beer, along with the sprigs of rosemary.

Push the can, open end first, into the chicken cavity. The trick is to balance the chicken so that it stands over the grill without falling over.

Cook covered for 1½ hours. Add charcoal as required to maintain an even, moderate heat.

The chicken is cooked when the juices run clean from an incision made in the thickest part of the bird, which is generally the thigh.

When cooked, carefully remove to a tray and allow to rest. Remember to discard the beer can before serving!

Char sui duck

When I moved from Perth to Sydney at the age of twenty-one, it really opened my eyes. There were many things I'd never experienced. I will always remember my first trip to BBQ King in Chinatown seeing the chefs hard at it and the rows of ducks hanging up, their ochre-coloured skin glistening from the glaze and drying to perfection. I have been trying to replicate the BBQ King chefs' efforts ever since, and love returning to the restaurant for the ultimate Chinese barbecue.

This dish is great served with steamed rice and Chinese greens. I suggest you cook two char sui ducks, as one is never enough!

SERVES 4

1 × 2 kg Muscovy or Chinese duck

CHAR SUI MARINADE

60 ml honey

60 ml dark soy sauce

1 teaspoon five-spice powder

2 garlic cloves, minced

2 cm piece of ginger, peeled and minced

2 tablespoons shaoxing rice wine or sherry

To make the marinade, place the honey and soy sauce in a saucepan and bring to the boil. Remove from the heat, add the remaining ingredients and allow to stand until cold.

Cut the duck through the back and flatten it (your butcher could do this for you). Pour a kettleful of boiling water over the duck 3 times, draining each time. Pat the duck dry, place in the marinade and leave to marinate in the refrigerator overnight, turning once or twice. Drain and reserve the marinade.

Remove the duck from the refrigerator and allow it to come to room temperature.

Prepare your barbecue for indirect cooking over a medium heat. Pour 4 cups of water into the drip tray underneath the grill, to help maintain moisture within the barbecue. If using a gas barbecue, place a wire rack over a large roasting tray and add 4 cups of water to the tray. Turn on the outer gas burners for indirect cooking.

Place the duck on the grill racks, put the lid on the barbecue and cook for around 1 hour. Maintain the heat at a medium Level by adding a handful of preheated coals when necessary. If the edges start to blacken or darken too much, just rotate the duck or leave the lid ajar to lower the heat.

Boil the marinade in a saucepan and reduce to a thick glaze. Just prior to removing the duck from the barbecue, brush it with the glaze and then allow to rest for 10 minutes before serving.

Daegi galbi: Korean pork chops

These spicy Korean pork chops rock! Koreans would usually use ribs but I like to make this recipe using streaky pork chops cut from the belly, as you get more meat than bone and a nice amount of fat adds to the lovely flavours. The spice mixture is quite hot, due to the kochujang (red pepper sauce), so it's best served with Kimchi (page 104) on the side to help control the heat. Once you start eating these chops it's hard to stop, mainly because the chilli starts to kick in if you do!

SERVES 6

10–12 streaky pork belly chops, skin removed, chops cut into 5 cm thick strips

MARINADE

2 onions, finely chopped

10 garlic cloves, minced

2 cm piece of ginger, peeled and minced

250 ml kochujang

4 tablespoons sugar

2 tablespoons soy sauce

3 tablespoons sesame oil

1 teaspoon freshly cracked black pepper

Purée the marinade ingredients then rub into the pork chops. Leave to marinate in the refrigerator for 4–5 hours or overnight.

Remove the pork chops from the refrigerator and allow them to come to room temperature.

Prepare your barbecue for direct grilling over a medium–high heat. Cook the pork chops for 8–10 minutes on either side.

Serve straightaway.

Char sui pork

Most people would be familiar with the lovely red strips of pork or duck hanging in the windows of Cantonese restaurants in Chinatowns around the world. It really is quite an easy thing to make yourself, and it's fantastic with simple greens and steamed rice. I've eaten it in Hong Kong with fried eggs.

The pork neck in this recipe is a cut from the top portion of the shoulder. It's good for this dish as it has a reasonable fat content.

SERVES 6

1.5 kg pork neck, fat left on
1 quantity Char Sui Marinade
   (page 176)

Cut the pork neck so it's a similar thickness all the way through (your butcher could do this for you). Immerse the pork in the cold marinade and leave to marinate in the refrigerator overnight, turning once or twice. Drain and reserve the marinade.

Remove the pork from the refrigerator and allow it to come to room temperature.

Prepare your barbecue for indirect cooking over a medium heat. Pour 4 cups of water into the drip tray underneath the grill, to help maintain moisture within the barbecue, topping it up as you cook. If using a gas barbecue, place a wire rack over a large roasting tray and add 4 cups of water to the tray. Turn on the outer gas burners for indirect cooking.

Place the pork on the grill racks, put the lid on the barbecue and cook for around 2 hours. Maintain the heat at a medium level by adding a handful of coals every hour. Turn the pork from time to time. If the edges start to blacken or darken too much, just rotate the pork or leave the lid ajar to lower the heat.

Bring the marinade to the boil in a saucepan and reduce to a thick glaze. Just prior to removing the pork from the barbecue, brush it with the glaze and then allow to rest for 15 minutes. Thinly slice the pork before serving.

Pork loin with bay and balsamic

The ancient Romans used to honour their heroes with wreaths of laurel leaves, so I am honouring the mighty pig with a barbecue and bay leaves! We used to make this dish at the River Café using top-quality rare-breed pork. I doubt you will find a better recipe.

The pork loin goes really well with Baked Beans (page 92), mixed with a handful of rocket.

SERVES 4

4 garlic cloves, chopped

1 sprig rosemary, roughly chopped

8 fresh bay leaves

150 ml balsamic vinegar

3 tablespoons olive oil

2–2.5 kg pork loin

1 teaspoon freshly cracked black pepper

Combine the garlic, rosemary, bay leaves, balsamic vinegar and oil.

Score the fat of the pork loin with a sharp knife in a crisscross fashion and season with black pepper.

Pour over the balsamic and olive oil mixture and leave to marinate for 2–3 hours at room temperature.

Prepare your barbecue for indirect cooking, although we will be using a direct grilling method to seal and colour the pork.

Cook the pork loin over direct medium–high heat, allowing the fat to caramelise and blacken slightly. Transfer to a lower indirect heat and cook, covered, for 25–30 minutes in a roasting or foil tray with a little of the marinade (make sure you include the rosemary and bay leaves).

Place the remaining marinade in a small saucepan and reduce.

Serve the pork drizzled with the reduced marinade.

Daegi bulgogi: spicy Korean pork

••••••   This popular Korean dish is eaten in the same fashion as the barbecued Bulgogi (page 151), with lettuce wraps, herbs, kimchi and spicy ssamjang sauce. The pork is marinated in a red pepper sauce called kochujang, as well as ginger, soy, sesame oil, garlic and sugar. Daegi is Korean for pork and bulgogi means 'fire meat', so this dish is known as 'pork fire meat'.

  I just love this style of grazing. Pork is just about the best meat to barbecue in the world, and the Koreans have nailed it with this number!

SERVES 6

500 g pork fillet, cut into thin strips

3 tablespoons soy sauce

5 garlic cloves, minced

1 cm piece ginger, minced

2 tablespoons palm sugar or light brown sugar

2 tablespoons kochujang

1 teaspoon chilli flakes

2 tablespoons rice wine

2 tablespoons sesame oil

sunflower oil

1 onion, finely sliced

½ iceberg lettuce

1 butterleaf lettuce or lollo rosso lettuce

3 tablespoons Ssamjang (page 23)

200 g Kimchi (page 104)

1 cup picked mint leaves

To make the bulgogi, combine the pork, soy sauce, garlic, ginger, sugar, kochujang, chilli flakes, rice wine and sesame oil. Leave to marinate in the refrigerator for a minimum of 30 minutes but no more than 1 hour.

Remove the bulgogi from the refrigerator and allow it to come to room temperature.

Heat your barbecue hotplate to medium–hot. Add a little sunflower oil to the hotplate and start to quickly fry the marinated meat. Add the onion and use a spatula to turn the meat. I like to cook on medium at this stage but most people prefer their pork well-done.

Transfer the daegi bulgogi to a serving dish, along with the lettuce, ssamjang and kimchi.

To eat, take a lettuce leaf and add a little ssamjang, kimchi and pork, top with mint leaves and roll up to make a wrap.

Chorizo roll from Borough Market

People queue up for ages at London's famous Borough Market to get their hands on one of Brindisa's barbecued chorizo and pepper rolls. The luscious, smoky chorizo picante is served up with sweet grilled peppers and spicy wild rocket. Team that with the awesome wooded flavour and sharpness of the sherry vinegar – the mere thought of it is making my mouth water!

Chorizo is great to cook on the barbecue, whether it's cured and thinly sliced to wrap around fish, or the fresh, spicy-hot chorizo that needs to be cooked before being eaten. There are many varieties of chorizo but they all have one thing in common: they are made from pork and get their flavour and colour from smoked paprika. A little bit of Aioli (page 31) is great with these rolls, and now you won't have to travel all the way to Borough Market to taste them!

SERVES 4

8 fresh chorizo picante, halved

1 bunch wild rocket

2 tablespoons sherry vinegar (Valdespino would be good)

4 ciabatta rolls or 1 Turkish loaf, sliced

extra-virgin olive oil

4 Fire-roasted Peppers (page 80)

salt

freshly ground black pepper

Prepare your barbecue for direct grilling. Place the chorizo on the grill and cook until nicely charred on one side, then turn over. There is a lot of fat in chorizo, so if the coals flame up, remove the sausages to a cooler part of the barbecue.

Dress the rocket with the sherry vinegar. Toast the ciabatta or Turkish bread on one side and drizzle with olive oil. Top with slices of roasted pepper and halves of chorizo, add some rocket and season with salt and pepper.

Close the buns and get stuck in.

Mexican suckling pig tortillas

 This is my all-time, pull-out-all-the-stops barbecue favourite. You have to get organised for this one, and you'll need a large barbecue. To make it easier, you could buy rather than make your tortillas. If you can't get hold of a suckling pig, use a shoulder from a younger animal. Putting on a barbecue like this will have your friends and family talking about it for decades! I like to use habanero chillies (or use six regular chillies if you prefer) and I marinate the pork in a classic Mexican adobo marinade – it goes well with fish or chicken too, but with pork it rocks!

SERVES 10

1 suckling pig or small pork shoulder on the bone (4–5 kg), lightly scored (ask your butcher to do this)

20 Tortillas (page 65)

2 quantities Guacamole (page 32)

2 quantities Shallot and Coriander Salsa (page 29)

1 quantity Refried Beans (page 93)

500 g sour cream

1 quantity Mexican Spicy Green Sauce (page 26)

ADOBO MARINADE

3 chipotle chillies, stems removed, soaked in hot water for 10 minutes

1 teaspoon smoked paprika

250 ml orange juice or 125 ml grapefruit juice and 125 ml lime juice

3 tablespoons tomato sauce

2 tablespoons dried wild oregano

½ teaspoon ground cumin

2 tablespoons white wine vinegar

2 teaspoons salt

½ teaspoon freshly ground black pepper

Place all the marinade ingredients in a food processor and blitz. Place the mix in a large plastic bag, along with the pork. Extract as much air as you can and tie the bag closed. Leave to marinate in the refrigerator for at least 4–5 hours.

Remove the pork from the refrigerator and allow it to come to room temperature.

Set up a large hooded barbecue with a spit. If you don't have a spit, prepare your barbecue for indirect cooking, starting at a relatively high heat. Pour 2 cups of water into the drip tray underneath the grill, to help maintain moisture within the barbecue, and keep topping it up as you cook. If using a gas barbecue, place a wire rack over a large roasting tray and add 2 cups of water to the tray. Turn on the outer gas burners for indirect cooking.

Place the pork on the grill racks, put the lid on the barbecue and cook at a medium–high temperature for 30 minutes, then lift the lid to cool. Cook for 4–5 hours with the lid down, basting with the leftover marinade from time to time. Maintain the heat at a medium–low level by adding coals every 30–40 minutes.

Once the pork is tender, remove to a large tray or board to rest. Fire up the coals while this is happening so you can heat your tortillas.

Carve the meat and serve in tortillas topped with guacamole, salsa, refried beans, sour cream and spicy green sauce.

FRUIT AND
SWEET THINGS

Not many people cook desserts on the barbecue. I hope this chapter will give you the motivation to either get up and finish the job or prepare some great dishes in advance to round off a wonderful meal. There's a simple syrup-soaked grilled pineapple served with a terrific Thai-inspired creation, a twist on an Aussie classic and a sensational summer pudding.

The thing about desserts is it doesn't matter how good the rest of the meal is, if your dessert is a flop, that's what your guests will remember. They won't take home the memory of those wickedly delicious pork ribs or that whole Thai-style fish. It will be the two-fruit trifle or the soggy tiramisu that tasted of onions from sitting in the refrigerator all night.

So do the right thing and have a go at making these easy, barbecue-friendly desserts.

Grilled pineapple with rum, ginger and lemongrass syrup

Ben, my pastry chef from the Atlantic Bar and Grill in London, met a Thai girl and travelled to Thailand to meet her family. He came back from his travels inspired by the wonderful food he'd experienced, and was particularly enthused by this recipe for grilled fruit.

The really exciting thing about this recipe is the sugar and salt condiment that's served with the fruit. I've come across this spiced sugar before, in David Thompson's kitchen at Nahm in London. The sweet–salty flavours created are so typically Thai. The recipe here is just a guide, as these things are best done according to personal taste. If you prefer more chilli, then add it. With the salt and sugar it's about finding the balance that's right for you, but I would recommend that you err on the side of sweet!

SERVES 4

1 pineapple, skin removed and
   cut into quarters, lengthwise

SYRUP

200 ml water

100 ml white rum

100 g sugar

3 cm piece of ginger, peeled
   and sliced

1 stick lemongrass, bruised

zest and juice of 1 lemon

zest and juice of 1 lime

1 dried red chilli

SPICED SUGAR

1 dried red chilli

2 teaspoons crystal salt

3 teaspoons caster sugar

To make the syrup, place all the ingredients in a saucepan and bring to the boil, making sure the sugar has dissolved. Remove from the heat and cool, then strain.

Marinate the pineapple in the syrup overnight.

To make the spiced sugar, pound the dried chilli and salt in a mortar until you have fine flakes of chilli. Add the caster sugar.

Prepare your barbecue for cooking on a medium–high heat. Place the pineapple over the heat and barbecue until caramelised, turning the fruit as required.

Once cooked, skewer the pineapple with bamboo sticks and serve with the spiced sugar as a dipping condiment.

Baked pears and apples

The humble pear and apple are often overlooked when it comes to barbecues. In the UK they are more likely to turn up in the form of perry (pear cider) or apple cider at your average backyard get-together – not that there's anything wrong with that!

Pears or apples stuffed with a lovely mix of dried fruit, nuts and booze are a real treat. They're wrapped in foil then thrown on the coals to cook while you're preparing the meat or other dishes. When you're ready to serve, accompany them with lashings of cream or ice cream.

MAKES 4

2 tablespoons raisins (or other dried fruit such as chopped dates)

100 ml brandy or rum

4 pears or apples (or a mixture of both), cored

100 g butter, softened

2 tablespoons soft brown sugar

2 tablespoons flaked almonds (or other nuts such as pecans)

2–3 grates of nutmeg to taste

¼ teaspoon ground cinnamon

Soak the raisins in the booze overnight or simmer together in a saucepan for 5 minutes and then allow to cool. Drain, reserving the liquid.

With a small knife, cut around the apples horizontally, about 1 cm deep.

Combine the raisins, sugar, nuts and spices, and stuff into the hollowed-out cores of the fruit.

Prepare your barbecue for cooking on a medium–high heat.

Wrap each fruit completely in foil twice and place next to the coals or above the heat source and cook for 40 minutes.

Serve while hot, drizzled with the reserved, reduced raisin liquid.

Barbecued peaches

Peaches are just about the perfect summer fruit. Grilled and accompanied by a smooth dollop of something simple like crème fraîche, they make the perfect finale to any barbecue, and they're so easy to prepare. Leave the peaches to rest for a little after they've been grilled, so their juices slowly ooze to make a wonderful syrup. Other summer fruit work equally well – try apricots, nectarines or even mangoes. The natural sugars will caramelise and you'll get a great sweet, smoky flavour coming through.

SERVES 6

6 ripe peaches (they *must* be ripe), halved and stoned

6 teaspoons brandy

2 tablespoons vanilla sugar

250 g crème fraîche to serve

1 tablespoon chopped mint leaves

Prepare your barbecue for cooking on a medium–high heat.

Place the peaches flesh-side down on the grill. Cook for 5 minutes, then turn the peaches 90 degrees so you get a crisscross pattern from the grill.

Turn the peaches over gently, sprinkle with brandy and a little vanilla sugar, and cook for a further 2–3 minutes.

Serve with a good dollop of crème fraîche and garnished with mint leaves.

Barbecued banana split

Caroline, a good friend of mine, gave me this cracking barbecue recipe. It's nothing revolutionary but it really appealed to me because I love the combination of bananas and peanut butter.

You need a sweet tooth for this one, so don't say I didn't warn you! Be prepared for the kids to start bouncing off the walls. This is a great recipe to make when you're going camping or having a barbecue in the great outdoors as you can prepare the bananas in advance and they travel well.

SERVES 6

6 ripe bananas, unpeeled

1 Snickers bar, thinly sliced

1 tablespoon runny honey

1 tablespoon crushed salted peanuts to serve

cream or ice cream (vanilla, or honeycomb if you're game) to serve

Prepare your barbecue for cooking on a medium heat.

Use a sharp knife to make an incision along the length of each banana, being careful not to cut all the way through.

Insert slices of the Snickers bar into the slit bananas, dividing the chocolate equally between the fruit. Drizzle with a little honey, sandwich the bananas back together and wrap in foil.

Place over the direct heat of the barbecue and cook for 10 minutes, 5 minutes on each side.

When cooked, unwrap the bananas, sprinkle on some crushed peanuts and serve with cream or ice cream.

Banoffee pie, my way

Banoffee pie is a true modern classic of English home cooking. It was invented some time in the 1970s, apparently in East Sussex, and its popularity in England is amazing. Therefore, it cannot be left out of an English barbecue experience.

The name comes from the pie's combination of banana and toffee, which is created by cooking a can of condensed milk. My variation on the classic uses the caramelised condensed milk to create a ripple effect, and the pie is finished with a drizzle of chocolate sauce. James Martin gave me the idea for this twist.

MAKES 8 PIES

PASTRY

350 g butter, cold
500 g plain flour
150 g icing sugar
3 medium egg yolks

FILLING

395 g can condensed milk
100 g good-quality dark chocolate, 70% cocoa content
200 g crème fraîche
250 g mascarpone
4 large bananas, sliced

CHOCOLATE SAUCE

100 ml cream
100 g good-quality dark chocolate, 70% cocoa content

Prepare the pastry by rubbing the butter into the flour and sugar until a fine crumb is achieved. Add the egg yolks and bring together until combined. Wrap in cling film and chill for at least 2 hours.

Place the unopened can of condensed milk in a heavy-bottomed saucepan, cover with water and simmer for 3 hours. Keep covered with water at all times, as otherwise the can could explode! Remove after 3 hours and allow to cool completely.

Roll out the pastry and line individual tartlet tins, leaving the pastry hanging over the sides. Cover the pastry with baking paper. Fill with rice and blind-bake for 20 minutes, until the pastry is set but not coloured. Remove the rice and continue to bake for 10 minutes, until the pastry is golden and crisp.

Allow to cool, then trim the edges of the pastry.

To make the filling, melt the chocolate and line the inside of each tartlet tin with a thin layer of melted chocolate.

Combine the crème fraîche and mascarpone in a bowl, and fold through the caramelised condensed milk to create a ripple effect.

Spoon the caramel into the tarts and top with slices of banana.

To make the chocolate sauce, heat the cream until just boiling. Remove from the heat, add the chocolate and mix until completely melted.

Drizzle the sauce over the pies and serve straightaway.

Mixed-berry meringue Swiss roll

This recipe is very simple to prepare. The crunch of the meringue and almonds, combined with the sweet sharpness of the berries, makes it an English pavlova! I first saw a fantastic cook called Mary Berry prepare the basic recipe for this dessert on a UK cooking show called *Daily Cooks*, and I've used it many times since.

I would recommend a gas barbecue for this one, and it also works well in a conventional oven.

SERVES 8

4 large egg whites
1 cup caster sugar
butter for greasing
50 g flaked almonds
icing sugar for dusting
mint leaves

FILLING

300 ml thickened cream
1 vanilla pod, split and scraped
50 g raspberries
50 g blackberries
50 g blueberries
100 g strawberries, quartered

Prepare your barbecue for indirect cooking over a high heat (200°C if you have a thermometer).

Whisk the egg whites with ¼ cup of sugar until just stiff. Add the remaining sugar and whisk until the mixture is stiff and glossy.

Grease a baking tray with butter and line with baking paper. Spoon the meringue over the paper evenly, then sprinkle with flaked almonds.

Place the tray between the heat sources for indirect cooking and close the lid. Cook at 200°C for 8–10 minutes, or until the almonds are golden. Keep an eye on things at this stage.

Open the barbecue and cool slightly. Close the lid, reduce the heat to around 160°C and cook for a further 15–20 minutes, or until firm to the touch.

Spread out a piece of baking paper, around the same size as the meringue, and dust with icing sugar. When the meringue is ready, turn it out onto the paper. Remove the baking paper from the bottom and allow to cool.

To make the filling, whip the cream with the seeds from the vanilla pod. Spread the cream evenly over the meringue, then scatter the mixed berries over the cream.

Starting from the long edge of the meringue, roll up tightly, using the paper to help lift and roll. Secure the roll tightly, leaving it wrapped in the paper, and chill for 45 minutes in the refrigerator.

Serve the meringue roll garnished with mint leaves and accompanied by additional fresh berries.

Sweet bruschetta

 These lovely fruity bruschetta remind me of a homemade fruit Danish. Serve with some clotted cream, crème fraîche or ice cream. They can be served as a dessert or as a fun breakfast or brunch, the choice is yours. It's also a great way to use up slightly overripe fruit.

SERVES 4

4 slices sourdough bread, sliced
  1½ cm thick
80 g butter plus 4 additional knobs
2 peaches, stoned and quartered
2 nectarines, stoned and quartered
4 apricots, stoned and halved
3 tablespoons soft brown sugar
80 ml brandy
1 vanilla pod, split and scraped

Prepare your barbecue for indirect cooking on a high heat, though you'll be toasting the sourdough on a direct heat.

Toast the sourdough slices over the direct heat of the coals or gas. Butter the toasted bruschetta on both sides and place on a roasting tray.

Toss all the fruit in the combined sugar, brandy, scraped vanilla pod and seeds. Allow to macerate for 10 minutes.

Divide the fruit evenly between the toasted bruschetta and drizzle with the juices. Top with small knobs of butter.

Place the tray between the heat sources for indirect cooking, close the lid and cook for 15 minutes.

When cooked, the fruit should be soft and lightly caramelised, and the edges of the bruschetta crispy.

Serve straightaway.

Summer pudding

If there's one thing the English do well it's puddings. And summer pudding has to be right at the top of the list. Using plain old white bread, plus loads of fresh or frozen berries, some nice red wine and sugar, it's thrifty!

I could not imagine a better end to a sensational summer barbecue than the sharp, sweet flavours of a summer pudding. It's best prepared a day in advance, which is nice because you can whip it out at the end of the meal with little fuss.

Accompany the pudding with some Greek yoghurt or crème fraîche.

SERVES 6

150 g caster sugar

50 ml water

1 vanilla pod, split and scraped

1–2 teaspoons freshly ground black pepper to taste

500 ml fruity light red wine (grenache or valpolicella are good)

600 g mixed summer fruit (strawberries, raspberries, blueberries, blackberries, etc.)

1 tablespoon chopped basil leaves

1 loaf sliced white bread, crusts removed

Sprinkle the sugar into a heavy-based saucepan. Pour over the water and stir to make a paste. Cook to a light golden caramel.

Add the split vanilla pod, some ground black pepper and the red wine, and bring to the boil. Simmer for 10 minutes, until reduced by half. Remove from the heat and gently stir in the fruit. Leave to stand until cold, then add the basil leaves.

Line a glass bowl evenly with the slices of bread, overlapping them so there are no gaps.

Fill the lined bowl with your cooled berry compote, then cover the top with overlapping slices of bread. Cover with cling film and place a plate on top to weigh the pudding down; the plate should be the same diameter as the pudding, but slightly smaller than the bowl. Refrigerate overnight.

When ready to serve, turn the pudding out onto a large serving plate or serve it straight from the bowl.

Damper doughnuts with marshmallows

This recipe was inspired by the television series *The Great BBQ Challenge*, in which aspiring grill masters were pitted against each other to vie for the title of Australian BBQ Champion. During one of the challenges, the contestants had to make a fire-cooked meal for a team of army training personnel. One of the recipes they came up with was doughnuts made from Damper, that great Aussie bush-cooking invention. With a little instruction from yours truly, their damper doughnuts turned out amazingly well.

These doughnuts are best served warm with vanilla ice cream.

MAKES 12

1 quantity Damper Dough
(page 52–3)

12 Marshmallows (page 213)

SYRUP

½ cup shaved palm sugar or
light brown sugar

zest and juice of 2 limes

125 ml dark rum (Bundaberg
would be good)

500 ml vegetable oil or
sunflower oil

To make the doughnuts, form the damper dough into small balls, about the size of golf balls. Pat each ball out flat and place a marshmallow in the centre. Fold the dough over and crimp the edges to seal the marshmallow inside. Allow to rest.

To make the syrup, place the sugar, lime zest, juice and rum in a saucepan and bring to the boil. Reduce until you have a thin syrup, then set aside.

Heat the oil in a wok over a medium heat, or on the side burner of your barbecue, until it reaches 170°C. You can test if it's hot enough by dropping a small amount of dough into the oil – it should brown in about 10 seconds.

Carefully place a few doughnuts at a time into the hot oil, and cook until golden and puffy. Allow them to drain for a few minutes on paper towels then place in the syrup so they soak it up.

Serve the doughnuts straightaway while they're warm.

Hotcakes

These are great for breakfast or you could serve them later in the day cooked on the barbecue. The combined flavour of bananas and dates, pecans and maple syrup is awesome. Serve them with cream or some great quality vanilla ice cream.

Hotcakes, or griddle cakes, are a classic American speciality, similar to big, thick pikelets. They are most often eaten for breakfast, served with maple syrup or bacon, and are generally cooked on a large skillet or in a griddle pan. This makes them perfect for the barbecue hotplate.

MAKES 8–10

300 g plain flour
1 tablespoon baking powder
1 tablespoon caster sugar
1 teaspoon ground cinnamon
½ cup chopped pecans (or nuts of your choice)
1 large egg
280 ml milk
½ cup chopped dates (Medjool dates are best)
butter
3 bananas, sliced
ice cream
maple syrup

To make the hotcakes, combine the flour, baking powder, sugar, cinnamon and half the chopped nuts. Add the egg and slowly pour in the milk until a thick batter is achieved that will drop but not be too runny. Mix in the dates and allow to rest.

Prepare your barbecue for cooking on a medium heat. Melt a little butter on the barbecue hotplate or in a nonstick pan. Half-fill crumpet rings with batter to get nice round shapes with depth. When bubbles and little holes appear on top of the hotcakes, turn them over to finish cooking.

To serve, remove the crumpet rings and top the hotcakes with sliced banana and a scoop of ice cream. Drizzle with maple syrup and scatter over the remaining nuts.

Lime and honey posset

A posset is a very simple, set cooked cream – an English version of panna cotta.

Possets are so easy to make and they taste sensational. They're great served with fresh fruit to counter the sweet creaminess. A classic posset is made with lemon juice, as you need the acidity to set the cream. You can also use lime, as in this recipe, or a combination of lemon, lime and orange.

SERVES 6

750 ml thickened cream
zest and juice of 3 limes
zest and juice of 1 lemon
175 g honey
1 mango, finely diced, to serve
6 sprigs mint

Heat the cream in a saucepan to 75°C. Remove from the heat and cool slightly to 65°C.

Add the lime zest, juice and honey to the cream and mix well to dissolve the honey; you should notice that the mixture thickens slightly.

Allow to cool, then pour into 6 cups or glasses. Place the possets on a tray, cover them with cling film and leave them to set in the refrigerator for about 4 hours.

Serve topped with mango and garnished with a sprig of mint.

Vanilla cheesecake with berries

Everyone loves a good cheesecake. Served with fresh berries, it's a great pudding to pull out at the end of a barbecue. Use good-quality Anzac or sweet oat biscuits, to make the base.

There is only one real cheesecake and that's a cooked one, prepared in the traditional American style. Set cheesecakes just don't have the same flavour and texture. This recipe is based on the method I learnt while cooking for Ruth Rogers at the River Café. I cooked quite a few meals at her home for some pretty amazing people and on one evening we cooked this particular dessert.

You can cook this cheesecake on a gas barbecue but it's safer to try it in the oven first. It needs to be prepared the day before you want to serve it so that it sets properly.

SERVES 8

80 g butter, softened
100 g biscuit crumbs
1 vanilla pod, split and scraped
400 g crème fraîche or sour cream
500 g Philadelphia cream cheese
250 g icing sugar, sifted
4 large eggs
400 g raspberries
extra icing sugar for dusting

Preheat the oven to 150°C or prepare your barbecue for indirect cooking. Heavily grease a 25 cm springform cake tin with butter. Throw in the biscuit crumbs and roll the tin around to coat the sides. The excess crumbs should cover the base in an even layer.

In a bowl, stir the seeds from the vanilla pod into the crème fraîche until smooth.

Beat the cream cheese with the icing sugar until soft and smooth. Add the eggs, 1 at a time, beating well after each addition. Fold in the crème fraîche mixture and mix thoroughly, then pour into the prepared tin. Bang the tin down on the bench to remove any air bubbles.

Transfer the cheesecake to the preheated oven or barbecue and bake on a baking tray on the lowest shelf for 50–60 minutes, until the centre just wobbles and the cake is just golden on top. Don't worry if the top doesn't colour very much; it's more important that the centre is cooked so that it just wobbles, but doesn't crack. Rest the cheesecake for at least 5 hours to cool and become firm.

When ready to serve, turn out the cheesecake, top with raspberries and a dusting of icing sugar, and slice into wedges.

Marshmallows

Who hasn't been camping and toasted marshmallows over the fire? They are just great. Kids love them, and now you have the recipe you won't need to buy them.

You can experiment with this recipe by adding different combinations of fruit and nuts and dipping the marshmallow in chocolate. You could even make your own rocky road! I love adding roasted hazelnuts or raspberries, and you could also try dried cherries or other dried fruit.

MAKES 24

150 ml still mineral water

450 g icing sugar

50 g liquid glucose

6 sheets leaf gelatine

2 large egg whites

1 vanilla pod, split and scraped

200 g cornflour

200 g additional icing sugar

Place the water, sugar and glucose in a saucepan and bring to the boil.

Soak the leaf gelatine in cold water for around 5 minutes or until soft, then squeeze out the excess liquid and dissolve in the syrup.

Whisk the egg whites with the vanilla seeds until they have soft peaks and are white in colour. Start pouring the syrup into the egg whites and continue to whisk until stiff and doubled in volume and the mixture is cool. Whip until cooled to room temperature (around 10–15 minutes).

Combine the cornflour and additional icing sugar, and dust a tray covered in baking paper with the mixture. Fill a piping bag with the egg white mixture and pipe marshmallows the size of ping-pong balls onto the tray.

Dust the tops of the marshmallows well with more of the cornflour and icing sugar mixture and let them stand for 4 hours until completely set. If you let them stand overnight they will go slightly crusty, which is fine.

The marshmallows will keep for 1 week if stored in an airtight container.

DRINKS

This book is a celebration of barbecues

and the fantastic food that can be prepared on them – but what is a celebration without a drink? For that matter, what's a barbecue without a drink? Answer: a job!

These suggestions are by no means typical of any particular barbecue style. They are the drinks I love to make – and obviously imbibe – and want to share with you. Some are reasonably friendly, while others need to be consumed with caution. Long on flavour and big on refreshment, they're all perfect for those long, warm afternoons around the barbecue.

I must point out that I advocate responsible barbecuing, and would advise that any major consumption of alcohol is best left until after the cooking is done. Having too many drinks while you're cooking is a bit like driving under the influence – it affects your judgement and ability to react, leaving you vulnerable to possible barbecue calamity.

Don't say I didn't warn you. The barbecue police are watching!

Lemonade

My wife and kids always make jugs of homemade lemonade when we put on a Vietnamese barbecue in our backyard. Lemonade is certainly not traditionally associated with Vietnamese food, but it's a refreshing drink and it goes so well with spicy Asian flavours.

SERVES 5

juice of 5 unwaxed lemons
zest of 1 unwaxed lemon
1 cup golden caster sugar or plain caster sugar
ice cubes
lemon slices

Combine the lemon juice and zest with the caster sugar until the desired level of sweetness is achieved. Stir until the sugar is dissolved.

Place ice cubes in tall glasses and pour over the lemon and sugar syrup.

Add water to taste, and stir to dilute.

Garnish with thin slices of lemon, and serve straightaway.

Rustie's Caribbean cooler

I get to work with some fantastic people on TV. One person who is larger than life is Rustie Lee. She came up with this recipe and I thought it would make the perfect barbecue drink. If you want to enjoy it, without the white rum, replace the spirit with water.

Rustie is from the Caribbean so it makes sense that this drink would go well with Jerked Chicken (page 168–9) or even the Mexican Suckling Pig Tortillas (page 186). Anything with a bit of spice!

MAKES 1.5 LITRES

250 g ripe or overripe strawberries
zest and juice of 2 limes
100 ml white rum
100 ml maple syrup
1 litre ginger ale
crushed ice
lime slices
quartered strawberries
mint leaves

Place the strawberries, lime zest, juice and rum in a blender. Pulse to combine.

Add the maple syrup and ginger ale, and stir.

Pour into glasses over crushed ice. Garnish with slices of lime, quartered strawberries and some mint leaves.

Serve straightaway.

Caipirinha

I have worked with a lot of Brazilians over the years, and if there's one thing I've discovered it's that they love a barbecue.

This is probably one of the most famous drinks to come out of Brazil, and it tastes sensational! It's made with cachaça, a spirit made from sugar-cane juice, combined with the refreshing flavours of lime and good sugar.

SERVES 1

2 teaspoons soft brown sugar
½ juicy lime
crushed ice
50 ml cachaça

Muddle the sugar and lime in the bottom of a glass tumbler.

Fill the glass with crushed ice and stir.

Pour over the cachaça and stir again.

Remember to sip!

Dark and stormy

This Cuban concoction is a cocktail classic, generally made with dark rum. It's a fantastic mix of spicy ginger beer, sweet dark rum and sour lime that's perfect on a hot summer's day and goes down a treat with spicy Jerked Chicken (page 168–9) or some finger-licking Barbecued Sticky Ribs (page 154–9).

SERVES 1

½ lime
crushed ice
50 ml Bundaberg rum or another dark rum
100 ml ginger beer
lime slices

Squeeze the lime over crushed ice.

Pour over the dark rum and ginger beer.

Garnish with a few slices of lime and stir.

Mojito

The mojito is a classic Cuban cocktail – long, cool and sexy, and just perfect for a barbecue. The wonderful balance of sweet and sour flavours pairs really well with the smoky, sticky flavour of Barbecued Sticky Ribs (page 154–5), Char Sui Duck (page 176) or Char Sui Pork (page 179).

SERVES 1

1 tablespoon soft brown sugar

½ lime, cut into wedges

8 mint leaves

crushed ice

50 ml Havana Club white rum

15 ml seven-year-old Havana Club rum

Muddle the sugar, lime wedges and mint leaves in a highball glass. Fill the glass with crushed ice.

Pour the white rum over the ice and mix thoroughly.

Float the dark rum over the top.

Drink straightaway.

Margarita

While filming a television series in Perth, we found ourselves discussing the merits of good tequila. Levon, one of the crew, boasted that he had, and I quote, 'the best margarita recipe in the world'. Well, Levon, it's pretty damned good, so I have paid it homage by including it here for all to try. I think I prefer mine shaken over ice and strained but you can try it as you like – frozen or just over ice, it's bloody good.

This mix can make as much or as little as you like. It's pretty straightforward: for two drinks, use 60 ml of alcohol and then do the maths. If you want a frozen margarita, fill the glasses with ice to measure, then blitz the ice with the booze in a blender and pour it back into the glasses. For a chilled drink, just shake the alcohol with the ice and strain it back into the glasses.

SERVES 2

30 ml gold tequila
15 ml silver tequila
15 ml Cointreau
juice of 1 lime
15 ml lime cordial
pinch of salt
crushed ice

Combine the liquids and pinch of salt in a shaker or blender, depending on whether you are making chilled or frozen drinks.

Measure the ice to fill each glass and add to the shaker or blender. For chilled drinks, just use the ice from 1 glass.

Shake or blend the cocktail until thoroughly mixed and divide between glasses.

If making chilled drinks, dip the rims in fine table salt before pouring the cocktail.

Pimm's

This is a classic English summertime drink and a wonderful way to start a barbecue. It celebrates the best things about an English summer: strawberries, cool cucumbers and the slight bitterness of the Pimm's – or is that just the taste left in the Poms' mouths from losing at the cricket every summer!

Pimm's is one of those drinks that goes with most food, but its cooling effect particularly suits spicy dishes. I like to drink it with Peri-Peri Chicken (page 172).

MAKES 2 LITRES

100 g strawberries, halved or
   quartered
1 orange, sliced
1 lemon, sliced
1 large apple, diced
½ cucumber, sliced
ice cubes
500 ml Pimm's
1.5 litres lemonade
1 cup mint leaves

Combine the fruit and cucumber with plenty of ice in a large jug or punch bowl.

Pour in the Pimm's and lemonade.

Stir to mix and then add the mint leaves.

Serve straightaway.

Southern Cross Pimm's

I love this combination – it's such a cool, refreshing mix – though I think this is probably the only way one should ever ingest the New Zealand fruit feijoas. That why I call this cocktail the Southern Cross Pimm's!

You need to watch out for this one: it grabs you and takes you on a journey!

SERVES 1

ice cubes
1 cucumber, cut into thin slices or sticks
¼ lime
mint leaves
50 ml Feijoa Vodka (made by 42 Below)
lemonade

Place plenty of ice cubes in a glass, along with the cucumber, lime (give it a squeeze) and some mint leaves.

Pour over the vodka, top with lemonade and stir.

Serve straightaway.

CHEF'S NOTES

Most ingredients in *Outdoor* can be bought from general supermarkets or speciality stores. I always try to buy the best ingredients I can afford, which doesn't mean that everything always has to be organic or that meat needs to be sourced from rare breeds reared by monks in virgin forests! But if it's possible for me to buy the best, I will.

CHEESE Cheese, whether parmesan or cheddar, is always freshly grated.

CHICKEN Chicken is preferably free range and organic.

CITRUS ZEST Lemon or citrus zest is finely grated.

CREAM Cream is generally pouring cream with a fat content of 35%.

EGGS Eggs are standard medium 55 g and preferably free range and organic.

FLOUR Plain flour is preferably organic. Masa harina is a speciality flour made from maise. It's not at all like cornflour. You could use semolina as a replacement but the flavour would be different. Atta flour is an Indian speciality flour made from split peas.

GARLIC AND GINGER PASTE Garlic and ginger paste is made by simply puréeing garlic or ginger in a food processor with a little oil to loosen to a smooth consistency.

GARLIC AND ONION FLAKES These can be made at home. Finely slice garlic and onion, then gently fry them in some oil at about 150°C until golden. Leave to cool on paper towels. This may seem a little laborious but the results are much better than using flakes you've bought from the supermarket. The pre-cooked flakes you can buy from Chinese supermarkets are okay, but I would advise against buying the Western ones in small glass jars unless absolutely pressed for time.

HERBS I generally use fresh herbs but I've noted where dried herbs are necessary (for example, in rubs and a few sauces). If I have any leftover hard herbs like thyme, sage, rosemary, curry leaves or lime leaves, I like to dry them by simply tying them together with string and hanging them up to dry in a cool, dry place and then storing them in airtight containers. When it comes to oregano, I prefer to use the flowering dried variety, which I call wild oregano.

SALT Maldon is the most widely available quality sea salt but any good-quality crystal salt is fine. Rock salt is always coarse unless otherwise stated. Salt flakes are the same as crystal salt.

TOMATO SAUCE Tomato sauce is generally good old Heinz.

VANILLA SUGAR You can make your own vanilla sugar by storing used dried vanilla pods in sugar over a period of time to allow the flavour to infuse. Alternatively, blend 1 pod with 2 cups of sugar. Either way, vanilla sugar needs to be stored in an airtight container.

Index

Adobo marinade 186

Aioli 31

almonds

  Lemon, honey, thyme and almond dressing 79

Aloo gobi parathas: roti breads stuffed with cauliflower and potatoes 57

anchovy

  Anchovy and rosemary sauce 15

  Marinated fire-roasted peppers with anchovies 80

  Marinated fire-roasted peppers with anchovies bruschetta 45

  Salsa di dragoncella 21

  Salsa verde 17

apples

  Baked pears and apples 195

  Coleslaw 101

Argentinian asado 140

artichokes

  Artichokes with lemon, honey, thyme and almond dressing 79

  Coal-baked artichokes 76

Asparagus robatayaki 72

Aussie steak sandwich 144

avocado

  Guacamole 32

Baba ganoush 74

bacon

  Baked sweet potatoes with speck, cloves and maple syrup 83

  Barbecued corn with bacon and chilli butter 89

  Coppa di Parma and blue cheese polenta 63

Moreton Bay bugs with figs and pancetta kebabs 129

Baked beans 92

Baked pears and apples 195

Baked sweet potatoes 82

Baked sweet potatoes with green chilli and lemon oil 82

Baked sweet potatoes with speck, cloves and maple syrup 83

Balsamic rosemary onions 90

bananas

  Banoffee pie, my way 199

  Barbecued banana split 197

  Hotcakes 206

Barbecued banana split 197

Barbecued corn with bacon and chilli butter 89

Barbecued peaches 196

Barbecued pepper chicken curry 173

Barbecued rib of beef 152–3

Basic barbecue sauce 14

basil

  Basil mayonnaise 31

  Mozarella with peppers and basil bruschetta 45

  Panzanella 98

  Salsa verde 17

beans, dried

  Baked beans 92

  Caribbean rice and peas 91

  Refried beans 93

  Spiced red bean salad 100

beans, fresh

  Som tam: green papaya salad 105

beef

  Aussie steak sandwich 144

  Barbecued rib of beef 152–3

  Beef brisket Texas-style 148

Bistecca alla fiorentina 146–7

Bulgogi: Korean barbecued beef 151

Bun bo: Vietnamese grilled beef and noodle salad with lemongrass 157

Malay satay beef 149

Thai beef salad 156

The perfect steak 142–3

beer

  Beef brisket Texas-style 148

  Bender's beer-can chicken 175

  Drunken crabs 131

  Singapore chilli crabs 132

Ben's childhood fish 112

berries

  Mixed-berry meringue Swiss roll 200

  Summer pudding 203

  Vanilla cheesecake with berries 210

Bistecca alla fiorentina 146–7

bread

  Cheesy garlic bread 51

  Panzanella 98

  Salsa di dragoncella 21

  Summer pudding 205

  Sweet bruschetta 204

  see also bread doughs; bruschetta; sandwiches

bread doughs

  Chapatti 56

  Damper 52–3

  Focaccia 54

  Naan 59

  Quesadillas 64

  Roti dough 57

  Tortillas 65

British beef wash 153

Bruschetta 44

  Fig, mint and mozzarella bruschetta 48

  Marinated fire-roasted peppers with anchovies bruschetta 45

  Marinated olives and mozzarella bruschetta 45

  Mozarella with peppers and basil bruschetta 45

  Simple tomato and garlic bruschetta 48

  Sweet bruschetta 202

Bulgogi: Korean barbecued beef 151

Bun bo: Vietnamese grilled beef and noodle salad with lemongrass 157

Butter, chilli and cheese polenta 63

butters

  Chilli butter 89

  Herb butter 126

cabbage

  Coleslaw 101

  Kimchi 104

Caipirinha 219

Cajun rub 36

Cajun spice 36

Cape Town kingfish fillets 113

capsicum see peppers

Caribbean jerked red fish 125

Caribbean rice and peas 91

carrots

  Carrot salad 102

cauliflower

  Aloo gobi parathas: roti breads stuffed with cauliflower and potatoes 57

celery

  Celery salt 35

Coleslaw 101
Shaved fennel and celery
salad 85
Chapatti 56
Char sui duck 176
Char sui marinade 176
Char sui pork 179
cheese
Butter, chilli and cheese
polenta 63
Cheese quesadillas 64
Cheesy garlic bread 51
Coppa di Parma and blue
cheese polenta 63
Fig, mint and mozzarella
bruschetta 48
Grilled haloumi 75
Grilled tomatoes and
cottage cheese 97
Marinated olives and
mozzarella bruschetta
45
Mozarella with peppers
and basil bruschetta 45
Pamplona chicken 170–1
Polenta 60
Zucchini and cheese
quesadillas 64
Chermoula marinade 162
chicken
Barbecued pepper
chicken curry 173
Bender's beer-can
chicken 175
Gai yang: Thai barbecued
chicken 165
Jerked chicken 168–9
Paella 124
Pamplona chicken 170–1
Peri-peri chicken 172
Tandoori chicken 166–7
chillies
Adobo marinade 186
Baked sweet potatoes
with green chilli and
lemon oil 82
Barbecued pepper
chicken curry 173

Butter, chilli and cheese
polenta 63
Chilli butter 89
Chipotle salt 37
Harissa 22
Indian spice-crusted fish
119
Jerk spice 112
Jerked chicken 168–9
Mexican spicy green
sauce 26
Peri-peri marinade 172
Red marinade 167
Scallops with sweet chilli
jam 130
Singapore chilli crabs 132
Som tam: green papaya
salad 105
Spiced sugar 194
Ssamjang 23
Sweet chilli sauce 26
Thai sweet chilli jam 27
Chimichurri 20
Chipotle salt 37
Chorizo roll from Borough
Market 183
Classic barbecue rib rub
33
Classic barbecued sticky
ribs 154–5
Coal-baked artichokes 76
coconut
Caribbean rice and peas
91
Gai yang: Thai barbecued
chicken 165
Satay sauce 28
Coleslaw 101
Coppa di Parma and blue
cheese polenta 63
coriander
Carrot salad 102
Gai yang: Thai barbecued
chicken 165
Jerk spice 112
Shallot and coriander
salsa 29
Spiced red bean salad 100
Whole fish Thai style 110

corn
Barbecued corn with
bacon and chilli butter
89

Daegi bulgogi: spicy
Korean pork 182
Daegi galbi: Korean pork
chops 178
Damper 52–3
Damper doughnuts with
marshmallows 205
Dark and stormy 219
desserts
Baked pears and apples
195
Banoffee pie, my way 199
Barbecued banana split
197
Barbecued peaches 196
Damper doughnuts with
marshmallows 205
Grilled pineapple
with rum, ginger and
lemongrass syrup 192
Hotcakes 206
Lime and honey posset
209
Mixed-berry meringue
Swiss roll 200
Summer pudding 203
Sweet bruschetta 202
Vanilla cheesecake with
berries 210
dressings
for Grilled verdure miste
70
Lemon, honey, thyme
and almond dressing
79
Nuoc cham 29
see also mayonnaise;
sauces
drinks
Caipirinha 219
Dark and stormy 219
Lemonade 218
Margarita 222
Mojito 220

Pimm's 223
Rustie's Caribbean cooler
218
Southern Cross Pimm's
225
Drunken crabs 131

eggplant
Miso eggplant robatayaki
73
Baba ganoush 74

fennel
Marinated olives 99
Shaved fennel and celery
salad 85
Squid stuffed with fennel
and black pudding 134
figs
Fig, mint and mozzarella
bruschetta 48
Kiwi barbecued trout
with figs 118
Moreton Bay bugs with
figs and pancetta
kebabs 129
Fire-roasted peppers 80
fish
Ben's childhood fish 112
Cape Town kingfish
fillets 113
Caribbean jerked red
fish 125
Indian spice-crusted
fish 119
Kiwi barbecued trout
with figs 118
Miso-blackened fish
fillets 116
Salt-crusted fish in coals
115
Sicilian sardines in oil
122
Snowy Morrison's hot
smoked salmon 121
Whole fish Thai style 110
see also seafood
Focaccia 54

fruit
  Baked pears and apples 195
  Grilled pineapple
    with rum, ginger and
    lemongrass syrup 192
  Pimm's 223
  Sweet bruschetta 202
see also specific fruit

Gai yang: Thai barbecued
  chicken 165
garlic
  Aioli 31
  Barbecued pepper chicken
    curry 173
  Cajun spice 36
  Cheesy garlic bread 51
  Garlic, lemon and green
    peppercorn salt 38
  Simple tomato and garlic
    bruschetta 48
ginger
  Orange and ginger ketchup
    15
  Rum, ginger and
    lemongrass
    syrup 192
  Glaze for classic barbecued
    sticky ribs 154–5
  Grilled haloumi 75
  Grilled lobsters 126
  Grilled pineapple with rum,
    ginger and lemongrass
    syrup 192
  Grilled rabbit Trapani-style
    163
  Grilled tomatoes and cottage
    cheese 97
  Grilled verdure miste 70
  Guacamole 32

Harissa 22
herbs
  Chermoula marinade 162
  Grilled verdure miste 70
  Herb butter 126
  Salsa verde 17
see also specific herbs

honey
  Char siu marinade 176
  Honey mustard
    mayonnaise 144
  Lemon, honey, thyme and
    almond dressing 79
  Lime and honey posset 209
Hotcakes 206

Indian spice-crusted fish 119

Jerk spice 112
Jerked chicken 168–9

Kimchi 104
Kiwi barbecued trout with
  figs 118

lamb
  Lamb burgers 159
  Lamb kofte 158
  Lamb shish with
    chermoula 162
Lemonade 218
lemongrass
  Bun bo: Vietnamese grilled
    beef and noodle salad
    with lemongrass 157
  Grilled pineapple with
    rum, ginger and
    lemongrass syrup 192
lemons
  Baked sweet potatoes with
    green chilli and lemon
    oil 82
  Garlic, lemon and green
    peppercorn salt 38
  Lemon, honey, thyme and
    almond dressing 79
  Lemonade 218
  Salt-crusted fish in coals
    115
Lettuce cups 151, 182
lime
  Caipirinha 219
  Dark and stormy 219
  Lime and honey posset 209
  Margarita 222

Mexican spicy green sauce
  26
Nuoc cham 29
Rustie's Caribbean
  cooler 218
syrup for Damper
  doughnuts 205

Malay satay beef 149
Margarita 222
Marie Rose cocktail sauce 31
marinades
  Adobo marinade 186
  Char sui marinade 176
  Chermoula marinade 162
  for Aussie steak sandwich
    144
  for Bun bo: Vietnamese
    grilled beef and noodle
    salad with lemongrass 157
  for Caribbean jerked red
    fish 125
  for Gai yang: Thai
    barbecued chicken 165
  for Indian spice-crusted
    fish 119
  for Jerked chicken 168–9
  for Malay satay beef 149
  for Whole fish Thai
    style 110
  for Whole pumpkin
    biryani 86
  Harissa 22
  marinade for Daegi galbi:
    Korean pork chops 178
  Miso marinade 23
  Peri-peri marinade 172
  Red marinade 167
Marinated fire-roasted
  peppers with anchovies 80
Marinated fire-roasted
  peppers with anchovies
  bruschetta 45
Marinated olives 99
Marinated olives and
  mozzarella bruschetta 45
Marshmallows 213
mayonnaise 30
  Aioli 31

Basil mayonnaise 31
Honey mustard
  mayonnaise 144
Marie Rose cocktail sauce
  31
meat see specific meats
  Grilled rabbit Trapani-style
    163
Mexican spicy green sauce
  26
Mexican suckling pig
  tortillas 186
mint
  Fig, mint and mozzarella
    bruschetta 48
  Mojito 220
  Pimm's 223
  Salsa verde 17
Miso eggplant robatayaki 73
Miso marinade 23
Miso-blackened fish fillets
  116
Mixed-berry meringue Swiss
  roll 200
Mojito 220
Moreton Bay bugs with figs
  and pancetta kebabs 129
Mozarella with peppers and
  basil bruschetta 45

Naan 59
Nuoc cham 29

olives
  Marinated olives 99
  Marinated olives and
    mozzarella bruschetta 45
onions
  Balsamic rosemary onions
    90
  Onion confit 144
  Shallot and coriander salsa
    29
  Thai beef salad 156
oranges
  Adobo marinade 186
  Orange and ginger ketchup
    15

oregano
  Adobe marinade 186
  Chimichurri 20
  Grilled rabbit Trapani-style 163
  Sicilian sardines in oil 122

Paella 124
Pamplona chicken 170–1
pancetta *see* bacon
Panzanella 98
papaya
  Som tam: green papaya salad 105
parsley
  Salsa verde 17
  Tabouli 103
pastry 201
peaches
  Barbecued peaches 196
  Sweet bruschetta 202
peppers
  Fire-roasted peppers 80
  Marinated fire-roasted peppers with anchovies 80
  Marinated fire-roasted peppers with anchovies bruschetta 45
  Mozarella with peppers and basil bruschetta 45
Pimm's 223
Peri-Peri chicken 172
Polenta 60
  Butter, chilli and cheese polenta 63
  Coppa di Parma and blue cheese polenta 63
pork
  Char sui pork 179
  Classic barbecued sticky ribs 154–5
  Daegi bulgogi: spicy Korean pork 182
  Daegi galbi: Korean pork chops 178
  Mexican suckling pig tortillas 186

Pork loin with bay and balsamic 181
potatoes
  Aloo gobi parathas: roti breads stuffed with cauliflower and potatoes 57
  Rustic Spanish potatoes 94
pumpkin
  Whole pumpkin biryani 86

Quesadillas 64
  Cheese quesadillas 64
  Zucchini and cheese quesadillas 64

Red marinade 167
Refried beans 93
rice
  Caribbean rice and peas 91
  Paella 124
  Whole pumpkin biryani 86
Robatayaki vegetables 72
rosemary
  Anchovy and rosemary sauce 15
  Balsamic rosemary onions 90
  Smoked salt and rosemary 39
Roti dough 57
rubs
  Cajun rub 36
  Classic barbecue rib rub 33
  for Beef brisket Texas-style 148
  for Classic barbecued sticky ribs 154–5
  Snowy's secret rub 121
see also salts
rum
  Dark and stormy 219
  Grilled pineapple with rum, ginger and lemongrass syrup 192

Mojito 220
Rustie's Caribbean cooler 218
syrup for Damper doughnuts 205
Rustic Spanish potatoes 94
Rustie's Caribbean cooler 218

saffron
  Paella 124
salads
  Bun bo: Vietnamese grilled beef and noodle salad with lemongrass 157
  Carrot salad 102
  Coleslaw 101
  Panzanella 98
  Shaved fennel and celery salad 85
  Som tam: green papaya salad 105
  Spiced red bean salad 100
  Tabouli 103
  Thai beef salad 156
Salsa di dragoncella 21
Salsa verde 17
Salt-crusted fish in coals 115
salts
  Celery salt 35
  Chipotle salt 37
  Garlic, lemon and green peppercorn salt 38
  Smoked salt and rosemary 39
see also rubs
sandwiches
  Aussie steak sandwich 144
  Chorizo roll from Borough Market 183
  Lamb burgers 159
Satay sauce 28
sauces, savoury
  Anchovy and rosemary sauce 15

Basic barbecue sauce 14
Chimichurri 20
Guacamole 32
Harissa 22
Mexican spicy green sauce 26
Nuoc cham 29
Orange and ginger ketchup 15
Salsa di dragoncella 21
Salsa verde 17
Satay sauce 28
Shallot and coriander salsa 29
Ssamjang 23
Sweet chilli sauce 26
Thai sweet chilli jam 27
see also dressings: mayonnaise
sauces, sweet
  Chocolate sauce 199
Scallops with sweet chilli jam 130
seafood
  Drunken crabs 131
  Grilled lobsters 126
  Moreton Bay bugs with figs and pancetta kebabs 129
  Paella 124
  Scallops with sweet chilli jam 130
  Singapore chilli crabs 132
  Squid stuffed with fennel and black pudding 134
Shallot and coriander salsa 29
Sicilian sardines in oil 122
Simple tomato and garlic bruschetta 48
Singapore chilli crabs 132
Smoked salt and rosemary 39
Snowy Morrison's hot smoked salmon 121
Snowy's secret rub 121
Som tam: green papaya salad 105

South American churrasco 140
Southern Cross Pimm's 225
Spice crust for fish 119
Spice mix for whole pumpkin biryani 86
Spiced red bean salad 100
Spiced sugar 194
Spiced yoghurt 162
Squid stuffed with fennel and black pudding 134
Ssamjang 23
strawberries
 Pimm's 223
 Rustie's Caribbean cooler 218
 Summer pudding 203
Stuffed gem squash 84
Summer pudding 203
Sweet bruschetta 202

Sweet chilli sauce 26
sweet potatoes
 Baked sweet potatoes 82
 Baked sweet potatoes with green chilli and lemon oil 82
 Baked sweet potatoes with speck, cloves and maple syrup 83
syrups 205
 for Damper doughnuts with marshmallows 205
 Rum, ginger and lemongrass syrup 192

Tabouli 103
Tandoori chicken 166–7
tarragon
 Salsa di dragoncella 21
Thai beef salad 156

Thai sweet chilli jam 27
thyme
 Lemon, honey, thyme and almond dressing 79
tomato
 Basic barbecue sauce 14
 Grilled tomatoes and cottage cheese 97
 Panzanella 98
 Simple tomato and garlic bruschetta 48
 Tabouli 103
tomato ketchup
 Glaze for Classic barbecued sticky ribs 154–5
 Marie Rose cocktail sauce 31
 Orange and ginger ketchup 15
 Singapore chilli crabs 132

Tortillas 65
Vanilla cheesecake with berries 210
vegetables
 Grilled verdure miste 70
 Robatayaki vegetables 72
 see also specific vegetables

Whole fish Thai style .110
Whole pumpkin biryani 86

yoghurt
 and cucumber dressing 173
 and mint dressing 159
 marinades 86, 149
 Red marinade 167
 Spiced yoghurt 162
zucchini
 Zucchini and cheese quesadillas 64

Acknowledgements

This particular book has been waiting for me to write it; I can't believe that it took me so long to get here. It's a style of cooking that has been part of my life since I was a kid. This is my first stand alone publication and I have to thank Julie Pinkham for believing in my idea and giving me the support of such a great team, Mary Small, Janet Austin and Ellie Smith (who have put up with my illiteracy, delays and excuses) and the rest of the team at Hardie Grant.

I could not have managed to write this book without the endless patience of my beautiful wife De-arne. She kept our kiddies from under my feet whilst I was twirling the tongs and hammering out recipes on the computer, as well as helping to clean up after barbecue sessions and parties. To Ruby, Herb and Cash my little ones for being my inspiration and joy. Craigy Kinder the main man with the camera for doing some of his best work for me and for being an awesome bloke, mate and surfing partner! His side kick and all round star and equally awesome camera man Rosco Picco Train! Sorry mate – had to do it! To Mandy Biffin, for her wonderful organisational and cooking skills, being the most relaxed and amazing person to work with. And a great cook. Thanks to Valli Little for putting me in contact with her, for which I am truly grateful.

Thanks to Nanette Backhouse for a great look and design, Jane Hann and Adele Snyman for a great styling and propping job which allowed me to get on with the job of barbecuing. The girls with the smoke and mirrors! For making me look half decent on the cover and wherever necessary: Samantha Theron (stylist to the stars and me) and Linda West (make up/magician) – love you guys. Dan Single at Ksubi for some fine threads, your support is appreciated.

The Suppliers: Barbeques Galore for all the hardware and support. What they don't know about barbecuing is not worth knowing and their service and support is second to none – it's the only place to buy a barbecue. Terry Wrights the finest butcher in the Eastern suburbs of Sydney and to Clayton Wright for his invaluable knowledge of all things meaty and Decosti for the freshest and finest fish. Nice one guys!

David, Erica and Jade Anderson for their friendship, support and hospitality. For all you have done for me, thank you. And all my mates who have been subjected to barbecue sessions at my house. Jamie Granger-Smith the only Scouser with a hyphenated name, Antonia, Zac and Benjie, John, Georgia and tribe (you are coming to Australia for a barbecue!). All the other Geordies we know, you know who you are! Those that enjoyed the pig session at the warehouse. Taxi drivers, KPs and chefs whom I have ever worked with, talked about food or consumed it with, you all give me inspiration.

If I have missed anyone I'll blame the editor for not picking it up in the second proof!